Lost Farms ᴜᴜury

R. McEwen Smith
and
M.T. Tonkin

First published in 1996 by
Redcliffe Press Ltd
22 Canynge Square Bristol BS8

© *R. McEwen Smith and M.T. Tonkin*

ISBN 1 900178 60 5

*This book is dedicated to all the families of
Henbury, especially the children.
Farmer Ray looks back with pleasure to the
visits to his farm gardens by children from
Henbury Court Infants School.*

British Cataloguing-in-Production Data.
A catalogue record for this book is available
from the British Library.

Typeset and printed by
The Longdunn Press Ltd., Bristol.

Contents

Preface

'Lost Farms of Henbury' was inspired by the impact of Henbury upon newcomers.

Access to this village is by roads flowing into and out of the city of Bristol. For instance, one directs visitors to 'leave the M5 at Exit 17, drive for a mile or so along the road to Bristol. When you see two high-rise flats, turn right at the roundabout. You are in Henbury!'

There are fields north of Henbury, and Blaise Castle Estate is to the west. But in all the other directions, Henbury is nowadays linked by built-up areas to the city centre.

When we newcomers had settled into our house, which is part of an ancient farmhouse, we began to look about us. We are townsfolk and Henbury had a different 'feel' about it from anything we had been used to.

We started to research our house, its occupants and its history, its place within the village. This led to an attempt to build a picture of farming in Henbury as it had been for many years before it was changed into a Bristol suburb.

One cannot and should not seek to 'put the clock back'. But an understanding of the roots of a place, like the roots of a family can bring pleasure and a proper sense of pride, as well as a feeling of continuity to present-day living.

M.T. April 1996

Fields of Norton, Westmoreland and
The Elms Dairy Farm

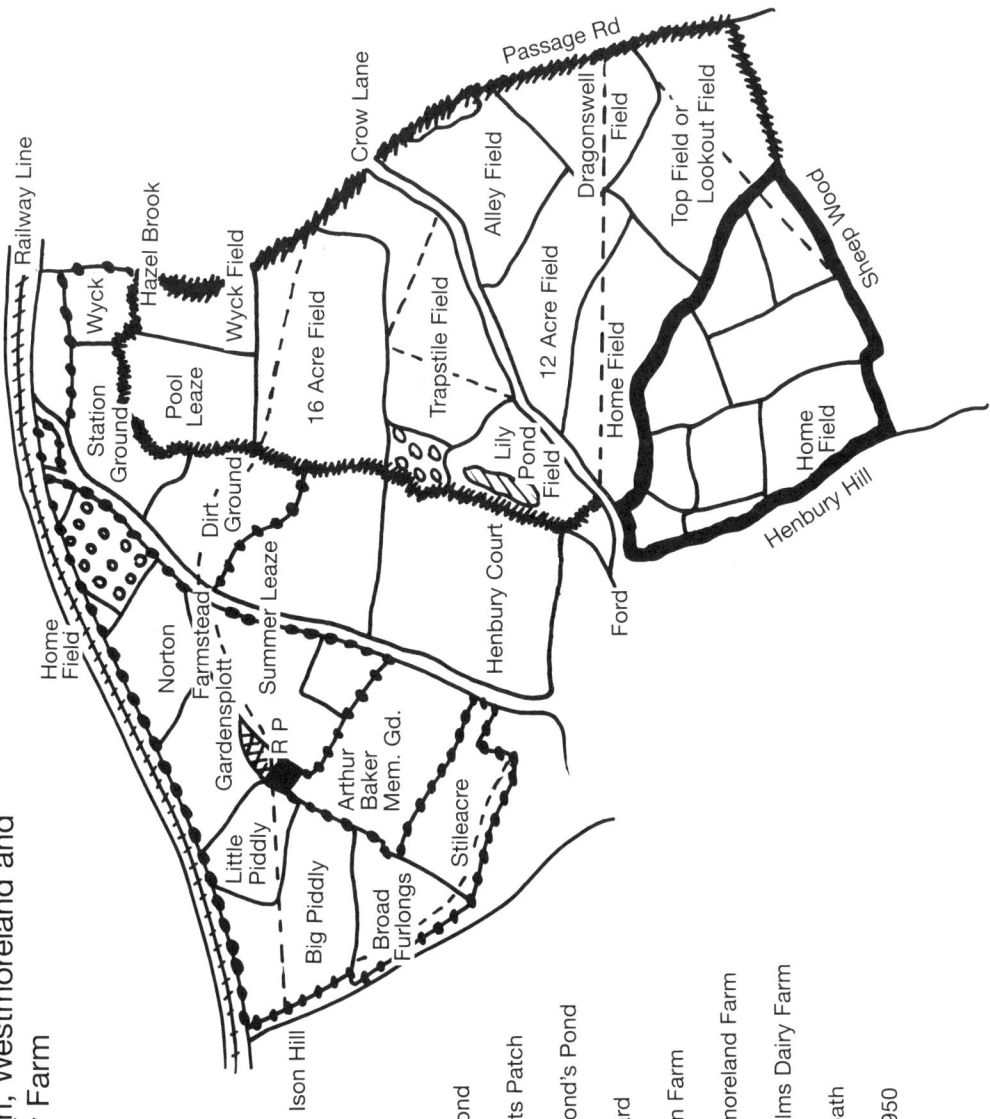

Railway Line

Home Field

Wyck

Hazel Brook

Station Ground

Pool Leaze

Wyck Field

Crow Lane

Passage Rd

Dragonswell Field

Alley Field

Top Field or Lookout Field

Sheep Wood

16 Acre Field

Trapstile Field

12 Acre Field

Home Field

Dirt Ground

Norton

Farmstead

Gardensplott

Summer Leaze

R P

Lily Pond Field

Henbury Court

Home Field

Henbury Hill

Ford

Little Piddly

Arthur Baker Mem. Gd.

Big Piddly

Broad Furlongs

Stileacre

Ison Hill

= Lily Pond

= Rabbits Patch

= Simmond's Pond

= Orchard

= Norton Farm

= Westmoreland Farm

= The Elms Dairy Farm

= Footpath

Before 1950

Introduction

We shall, in Part I, explore the last decades of Henbury as a farming village from 1930 to 1950 through the memories of Mr R. McEwen Smith and his family of Westmoreland Farm. In order to understand how and why an ancient rural community was so suddenly transformed into a city suburb, we shall first take a short glimpse at the history of the village, and the later policies and events that contributed towards the change.

The Gloucestershire village of Henbury had an ecclesiastical history dating from Saxon times, and, according to archaeological research, contained settlements dating back at least to the Iron Age.

Today, a walk round the village reveals St. Mary's Church as the oldest building in existence. This, in turn indicates the presence of a settled community as old as the church itself.

One reads in *St. Mary's Church, Henbury, A Brief History* that there are traces of Norman building modified and extended between the twelfth and fifteenth centuries. The earliest named vicar is Alwin in 1140. Parish records date back to at least 1538. From these can be gleaned some of the customs, employments and behaviours throughout the middle and later Ages of a vigorous village community ranging from the grand rich to the humble poor.

In 1930 it was evident that the earliest dwellings still standing originated from about 1600. Anything earlier had obviously been demolished. There is plenty of evidence of earlier grand houses having been pulled down. For instance, Henbury Manor was replaced in the late eighteenth century with Blaise Castle House. The Great House at the end of Station Road was finally demolished about 1821 and replaced with Henbury Court.

There was, according to the W.I. *A Guide to Henbury*, a vicarage 'of which there are records in the thirteenth century – on a site north of the church where the Vestry Hall stands today.' Henbury Awdelett was built on the foundations of an older house, 'Awdelett House'. So it is not difficult to imagine demolition of humbler dwellings when they became inconvenient, dilapidated or surplus to requirement. Ordinary people did not own their houses, many were living in tied cottages. Labour was cheap, and therefore simple buildings could be readily replaced.

Among the houses still remaining in 1930, were, in chronological

Henbury Village: 1921

Westmoreland Farm

Norton Farm

The Elms Dairy Farm

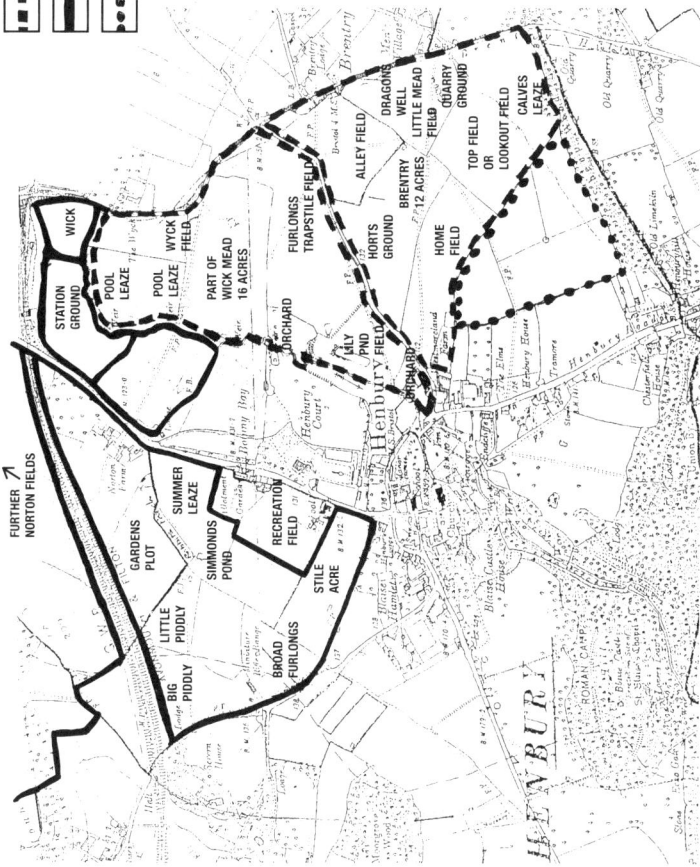

STATION GROUND

WICK

POOL LEAZE

POOL LEAZE

WYCK FIELD

PART OF WICK MEAD 16 ACRES

ORCHARD

LILY PND

HENBURY FIELD

ORCHARD

HORTS GROUND

FURLONGS TRAPSTILE FIELD

ALLEY FIELD

DRAGONS WELL

LITTLE MEAD FIELD

BRENTRY 12 ACRES

QUARRY GROUND

TOP FIELD OR LOOKOUT FIELD

CALVES LEAZE

HOME FIELD

FURTHER NORTON FIELDS

GARDENS PLOT

SUMMER LEAZE

SIMMONDS POND

RECREATION FIELD

STILE ACRE

BIG PIDDLY

LITTLE PIDDLY

BROAD FURLONGS

order, seventeenth century: Norton and Westmoreland Farmhouses, Fane Cottage, Close House, Sexton's Cottage, probably Westmoreland Cottage, and Henbury Awdelett. Probably most of the village shops came next. The Elms Farmhouse is thought by Robert Biggs to be Queen Anne – early seventeen hundreds.

Eighteenth century: there was a spate of building throughout the eighteenth century when, at the heyday of merchant enterprise, wealthy Bristolians sought rural retreats. Some houses of this period can be seen along Henbury Hill, and along Henbury Road between the Police Station and the shops. To a similar time belong Blaise Castle House, Severn House, Hill End and Henbury (old) vicarage. On a smaller scale from this period is the terrace of Sparside and Elm Cottages. By 1800, Telephone Cottage had been built.

Nineteenth century: as the century 'turned', Henbury Court was built, Blaise Hamlet, Botany Bay Cottages and Henbury Lodge. Further into this century appeared Hillside Cottage, Raglan and Alma Villas, the Post Office and Corner House.

Twentieth century: the Dower House was built in about 1900 and Ison Hill Cottages were about 1920. North Lodge was about 1902.

If one adds to all these houses a few more – two farmworkers' cottages at Dragonswell, Wyck House, Wyck Cottage, Beaconsfield, Applegarth, Chevening House, the Chalet and a few scattered cottages along the edge of Passage Road – this about sums up Henbury housing in 1930.

This detail is included so that it can be seen that between 1600 and 1930, the village had grown, changed and developed gradually as a residential area. It is also evident that the greater part of the land had remained park and farmland. This state of affairs was likely to remain so while ownership lay in the hands of a few wealthy families who enjoyed their rural way of life and status as landowners.

For example, until 1926 the Harford family owned Blaise Castle Estate as well as large areas of Westbury farmland. Fortunately, the Estate was then purchased by Bristol Corporation for use as a public park. In 1930, the Sampson-Way family still owned Westmoreland and Norton Farms. Mr. Langfield owned Henbury Court. The land of The Elms Dairy Farm was, at that time, owned by Mr Sommerville Gunn of Henbury House. Henbury was entirely rural and only 'organic' change seemed likely to disturb it.

Unfortunately for this peaceful outlook, in 1935 Henbury became part of Bristol and, like other neighbouring villages, achieved suburban status. The new status, in turn, made possible the dynamic change that occurred in 1950. Owing to a coincidence of social and personal circumstances – urgent need for post-war housing and the death of Major Sampson-Way – the farmlands were compulsorily purchased. In a few short years, extensive housing developments transformed the farming village into another dormitory suburb of Bristol.

The McEwen Smiths' story commences in Chapter 1 with William, who was the second generation of the family to farm in Henbury. He reminisces about his life and work, and about the high hopes he pins on his grandson to continue the family tradition.

William's death, coming shortly after this, marks the end of a somewhat gentle low-key farming life. In sharp contrast, his grandson, Ray, hard-working and ambitious, takes on the tenancy and rebuilds the farm as a thriving business. It is he who, so abruptly, has to face the end of his own and his grandfather's dream.

1 – 1930 William McEwen Smith

William was beginning to feel his age. He must be, he thought, because nowadays his hearth seemed ever more tempting. Here was his chair with the *Daily News* alongside. He would read of other men's exploits, thereby delaying the painful moment when he must heave himself up. Reports of the outside world were one thing, but his first concern must be with his own small part of it.

William's world was the village of Henbury. His personal responsibility concerned nearly one hundred and fifty acres, about one quarter of the entire village. In spite of his relatively small acreage, the land was good and sweet and had provided him with a contented life.

He had married many years ago and he and his wife had brought up four daughters and a son in moderate comfort. To his great grief, his wife, Annie died in late middle age. But now his son and three daughters were happily married with families of their own. Only Dorothy (Dolly) remained a spinster and she kept house for him.

Much later in his life, he had married again, a widow. They had made satisfactory arrangements, he and his wife and Dolly. His wife's house was rented out, she moved into the farmhouse and Dolly remained as housekeeper. Dolly seemed content and had many friends in and around the village.

William's mind that morning dwelt on his married children. They visited him from time to time with their families. There were seven grandchildren in all, lively and healthy, but only two would carry on the family name. His son, William George and his wife Nellie, born Collins, had two boys, Ray and Eric. They lived at Tickenham where William George had started as a tenant farmer on the Smyth Estate. Later, when the land came up for sale, he bought all four hundred acres, burdening himself with a hefty mortgage.

That big lad of his, Ray worked on his father's farm all hours after school and in the holidays from when he was quite a small boy. At thirteen, he had left school (with excellent exam results) and worked for his father full-time. He worked alongside the farm labourers, more than earning his keep, for he was a tireless and thorough worker.

William George, he knew, was a harsh taskmaster, and not one to lavish praise, but he trusted that boy with many responsible jobs, the boy would have to be content with that. William remembered that from

Round the ford

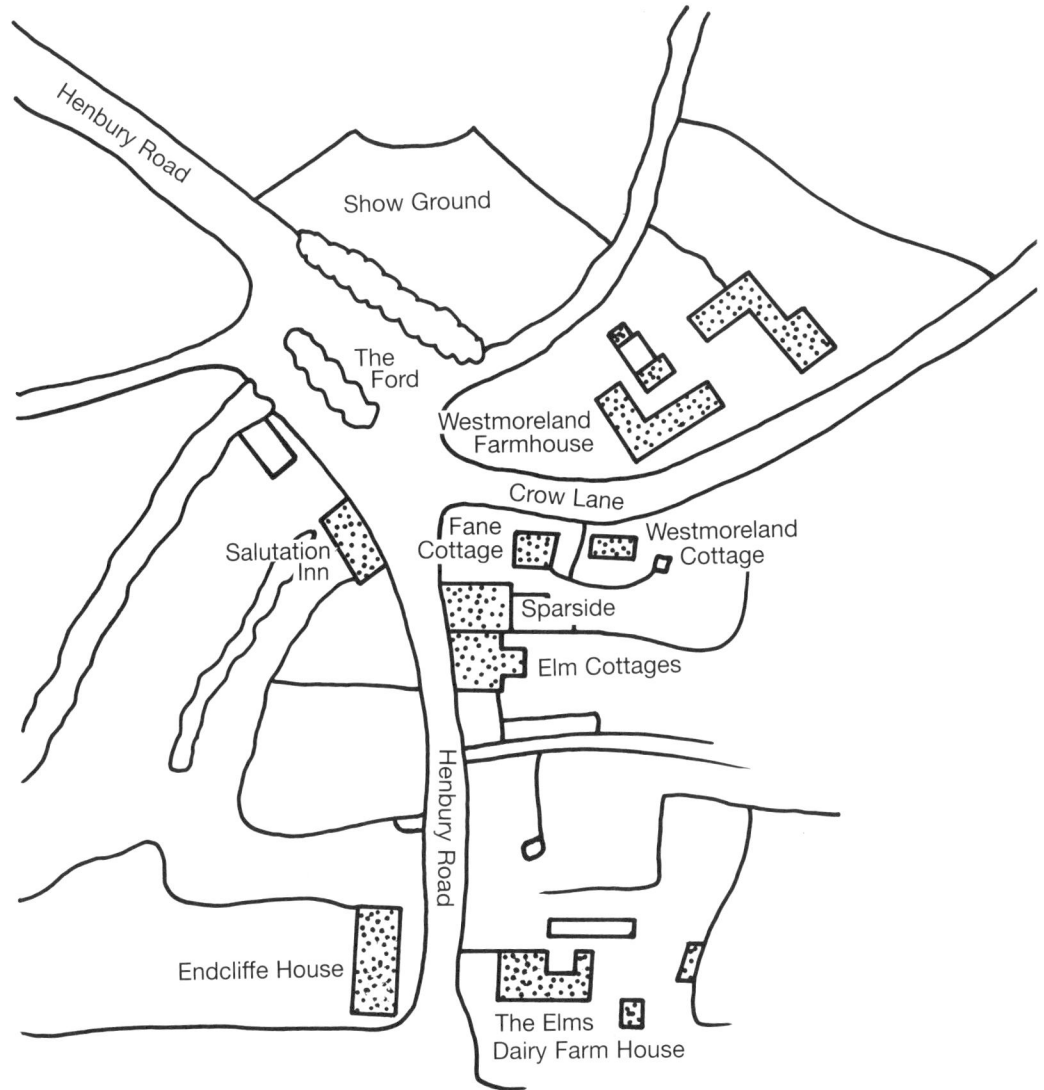

Henbury Road

Show Ground

The Ford

Westmoreland Farmhouse

Crow Lane

Salutation Inn

Fane Cottage

Westmoreland Cottage

Sparside

Elm Cottages

Henbury Road

Endcliffe House

The Elms Dairy Farm House

the age of about fourteen, his grandson was trusted with taking a wagon drawn by two or three horses into Bristol to fetch barley meal and Sharp's bran from Grace Brothers in Little King Street. And then he had to go on to Curtis's Mill in Feeder Road for linseed and cotton seed cake. He would load in all between 20 and 30 hundredweight at a journey. 'Yes,' he thought, 'he's a good lad, I've always enjoyed his company.'

A child visits Henbury's shops

William had his grandson over to stay as often as possible. His mind drew pictures of the boy at different times of his life. First, he saw the seven-year old entering the Windsors' sweet shop. On this occasion Mrs Maisie Windsor was out shopping and her husband, William who had a cobbler's business in the back room, emerged, mouth full of shoe tacks, large leather apron round his middle and big hands smelling of leather. Ranged behind the counter were rows of shelves laden with glass jars full of boiled sweets. Ray pointed to his chosen jar. The cobbler dived his hand into the jar, shook out the sweets on to the shiny brass dish of the scales, picked up and balanced tiny brass weights on the other side of the scales. Then he tore a cone-shaped paper bag from a string, poured in the sweets, gave the bag a twist and a swing and deposited it deftly into eager small hands in exchange for one penny.

When Ray was a little older, he made friends with Arthur Harvey, son of Herbert Harvey the plumber. All the shops and businesses seemed to fascinate him. The Windsors' shop was next to the Porter Stores. On the other side of the Porter Stores, Westminster Bank rented a room in a private house where their Branch opened for business 1-2 pm on weekdays. In behind this house, Rossiter ran an undertakers' business. Beyond this house lived plumber and taxi driver, Herbert Harvey.

Over the road was the Post Office run by Miss Margaret Stevens. This was William's favourite shop because it kept him in touch with the outside world through letters, telegrams, newspapers.

But he remembered another reason he liked it. To him, the Post Office was a novelty, for it had replaced older premises that were opposite the top of Hallen Road. The new Post Office had been built on the site of the Castle Inn by the Harford family. Next door, at the same time, they built the Corner House to accommodate their bailiff and his wife.

John Warburton, the postmaster and his wife then moved into the new premises. Margaret Stevens was their grand-daughter. The Porter Stores opposite had a roomy yard behind, where the mail cart used to park while mail delivery and collection was taken to and from the Post

Some of the buildings of Westmoreland Farm.

13

14

The old Salutation Inn.

The Salutation Bridge in the nineteenth century.

Office.

Ray, however, preferred the blacksmith's shop. He watched with awe while Jimmy Grigg shod horses and repaired farm and other machinery.

The Salutation and the ford

Sometimes William would take Ray across the road from his house to the Salutation Inn where Ruddock, a fairly new tenant would say, 'That's right, lad, run out to the back,' and the boy would go to the back room and sit on the bench by the warm Hastings boiler, sipping lemonade while William met his cronies at the bar. Ruddock was later to buy the Salutation.

To get to the Inn, they had to walk round the ford that more often than not was flooded. Their family had always kept ducks, geese and swans on the river. And here the birds could be seen when the ford was full, preening themselves. Horses stopped to drink there and it was a custom for Bristol people to come out on summer evenings to sit and watch and feed the birds. It was quiet and peaceful and a pretty sight, a noted beauty spot. 'All very well!' thought William, 'but when heavy rainstorms coincided with high tide, the farmhouse got flooded and damaged.'

Roaming the fields

On other occasions, the boy would be content to enjoy roaming the fields, playing in the brook, crunching apples in the orchard. As he grew older, he would help William and learn from him, for he loved being part of farm life. Farming goes back many generations on both sides of his family, and being brought up to it, it seems you either love it or hate it.

Now William was picturing his grandson at his present age of seventeen. He had heard talk of him deciding to leave home to join another farm in Gloucestershire. Well, he thought, 'here I am in Gloucestershire, too, with no chance of my son taking over here, not with the responsibilities of his own farm. I wonder now!'

William views his domain

Old William at last heaved himself up, walked through the hall, and along to the old part of his house. Then, passing through an ancient oak door, he emerged into the sunny courtyard. Across the yard stood a small stone building housing at one end the farm bakery, and at the other end the farm dairy. Even now, daughter Dorothy was hard at it in

16

the bakery, kneading dough for the bread. He thought of the cheeses stored in the upper room of the dairy, and the butter and cream produced by Dorothy's efforts.

Days that had gone by – they were very clear to him nowadays. He pictured the great family festivals at Christmas, christenings, weddings, when meats would be cooked in the large open-fire range with two ovens, housed in the bake-house near the baking oven. Home-grown cider flowed at these times and the farmhouse would be alive with his family and friends. The church bells were ringing just at this moment – perhaps they had reminded him of those past festive times. The bells made him feel secure and content.

William wandered across to the stables and barn. He'd always liked these good-looking buildings, grey dressed stone they were – on the front, anyway. Under the stone steps leading to the loft was the kennel for his dog to keep guard. Into the barn wall were set huge double doors up to the eaves. He was able to get fully-laden carts through them.

They knew how to build these things years ago! He'd been told they were Elizabethan, so they must have been built after the church lost its lands. So the tithe barn and stables must have been built by the Sadleir family, the lords of the manor, in order to collect the tithes, at that time owned by the Crown.

William's father had told him about these things. He also told him that at about the time he was himself born, tithing of farm produce had ceased, and rent had taken its place. After that, the old tithe barns were used in the general running of the farm.

William remembered another thing about his barn – that the thick wooden floor inside was at one time used for hand-threshing. At any event, the presence of dry grains for centuries in a water-tight barn had preserved the roof-beams strong and unblemished.

As the scurrying hens passed by, he glanced along the ridge running from Henbury Hill House eastwards. His fields ran alongside the fields of The Elms towards this ridge. His eyes took in the 'folly' or 'look-out' as the children called the ruin of the Lord Mayor's Chapel window. The ridge was his southern boundary as Passage Road was his eastern boundary. His fields ran both sides of the muddy track known as Crow Lane and stretched over to the Hazel Brook, and alongside its bank back to the farmhouse.

He owned a fine orchard about half-way along the brook, but most of his fields were used for grazing and hay. There were some good haystacks in those fields, stored for feeding his cattle in the winter months.

He made a mental inventory of his stock and reckoned he owned fifty five head of cattle including twenty five cows, rearing calves for meat

Post Office and Reading Room.

Henbury Church as William would have known it as a young man.

Vicarage life: games on the lawn and (below) a group of Vicarage servants in 1888.

and to replenish the herd. The meat cows and older calves were sold direct to local butchers who kept their own slaughter-houses at the back of their shops. One such was Elling of Westbury whose shop and house stood in High Street behind the fingerboard.

William next thought of his small flock of sheep, his pigs and poultry. The kitchen garden was strictly for home consumption. All this had sufficed to keep his large family. He was aware that he had never been ambitious, and had merely maintained what his father, a more driving man, had created.

Workers and friends

William looked again across Crow Lane, its rutted way leading only to the Old Crow Inn and Passage Road. The hedging on top of high banks needed continual maintenance, as did the ditches. He was lucky to have such good farm labourers.

Over the road was Westmoreland Cottage, a tied farm cottage, presently occupied by the Sampson-Way chauffeur. At the corner, in Fane Cottage lived his widowed sister, Annie Hort. Her girls and his daughters were friends, and had gone everywhere together – to church, to dances, to country shows. Years ago, they had got up a tennis club on Home Field, where they were joined by the Biggs of The Elms Dairy Farm and others.

The McEwen Smiths and the Biggs had always been on 'social visiting' terms together. And now a new generation of Biggs was coming along. Young Bobbie would sometimes put a raft on the brook behind William's house – and he was always welcome.

It seemed such a short time ago that Bobbie's grandparents, William and Louisa took on the tenancy of The Elms from Mr Levy Langfield, yet it was all of thirty years ago. They had had five children, all sons. Only eleven years after taking up the tenancy, William died. He was succeeded by his son, Stan, an ambitious young man of twenty four. Stan married Hilda Rowles from the Brentry farming family who were also good friends of William's family.

There were the Biggs, the Rowles and other neighbouring farmers in Brentry. There were also the Hignells, who had been in Henbury since 1917. They had become good neighbours and friends. Clem and his wife took over the lease of Norton Farm from Major General Sampson-Way towards the end of the war. Up till then, they had farmed in Lawrence Weston. They brought with them two small sons, Tom and Bob. As soon as they were old enough, the boys helped on the farm for there was much to do on a family-run business of 200 acres, mostly down to pasture.

The Village

To William, the village seemed changeless. The church was at its centre with the school and Close, the shops, the big houses, Post Office and Police Station. These were all at the heart of the village to which the villagers were drawn.

But, of course the village wasn't changeless. He himself had seen the Post Office change, the Charity School become the Elementary School. The Harfords had recently left Blaise Castle Estate with their large staff. People moved into the village and out of it. The old passed on (his landlord, the General had recently died), babies were born. What was it, then, that gave a sense of stability and continuity to Henbury?

Village dynasties

William's mind, now dwelling on happier thoughts, turned to the well-known village families. At the head of the list was the Major's family, the Sampson-Ways. Years ago, their ancestor, John Sampson had made money and, moving from Charlton Village, built Henbury Awdelett as his family home. For two hundred and fifty years the family had been there, buying up more land as time went on.

The vicarage family too, who had married into the Sampson family, had been there for a hundred years.

The Harfords had continued for three generations. John Warburton's family had already run the Post Office for more than fifty years. There were already two generations of McEwen Smiths.

His own family! William's thoughts returned to grandson, Ray. 'I must ask him to come and see me,' he mused. 'Though there is not enough turnover on the farm nowadays to pay another full-time farmer, he may be willing to "live in" and receive a small wage as the "heir apparent" to the tenancy.'

So, day-dreaming, he returned to his hearth, and his paper . . . Shortly after this, William took to his bed and remained there for many months, never again to leave it.

Henbury mothers and (below) a group of village lads, with the Windsors' shop on the left.

Royal Mail cart at the rear of the Porter Stores around 1900.

A bow rave wagon like that taken by grandson Ray to collect barley meal from Grace Brothers in Bristol. (print from Rural History Centre, University of Reading)

The Village Stores during the great winter, January 1947.

The front of Westmoreland Farmhouse.

William seen on the left of this group at daughter 'Babe's' wedding in the 1920s.

Ray as a child, with friend.

2 – Youthful aspirations

The news of William's death came as a shock to his family, even though he had been in failing health for some time. Now, there would be many decisions to make. Dorothy had spoken to her brother over the telephone and had offered to get in touch with the rest of the family. William George would make arrangements for the funeral and think about the future of the tenancy. He was an executor of his father's will and knew the contents.

He called his son, Ray to him and asked how far his arrangements with the Gloucestershire farmer had progressed. 'Nothing legally binding' was the reply. 'In that case, how would you like to manage your grandfather's farm between now and the sale?' asked his father.

The funeral is over

All formalities were over and done with. The boy on his horse looked forward with excitement to this next part of his life. The horse and he sauntered through Westbury Village after a fairly brisk pace from Ray's home in Somerset. The rider stopped his steed where the Trym in spate forded High Street. The young man looked at the ancient fingerboard as he had done on many previous occasions. He knew perfectly well where he should read 'Henbury' but he still thrilled as he heard himself say the name. He patted his horse's neck. 'This is where we turn off and climb Henbury Hill, old girl.' With a tired whinny, the mare responded to the rein and they turned left.

They passed the Rosery on one side and several large detached villas on the other. Then came farm fields left and right as far as the eye could see. Beyond the fields to the right, he could just make out a delivery cart driving along Passage Road from Westbury Village. Fields stretched north and west to Blaise Castle woods and the golf course, and over to Stoke Bishop and beyond.

As they progressed up Henbury Hill, two great houses appeared on the right. These were first, a Victorian mansion called Henbury Hill and, nearer the top, Henbury Hill House. Just over the summit and past Blaise Castle Lodge was Chesterfield House. Ambling to the top, the young man sat quietly on his horse and gazed down over his new home, Henbury Village. Strange how familiar it felt! He'd always enjoyed

Ray McEwen Smith with parents at the family farm in Tickenham.

staying with grandfather. Dad had worked him hard and had not found
time for play or talk as grandad had. But Dad had provided him with a
stern apprenticeship, and because of that he felt ready to launch himself.

It was a hazy autumn day, warm and mellow, and from his vantage
point, he could see his village – and what he couldn't actually see, his
mind's eye supplied.

Henbury Village was a compact, small domain bounded so
distinctively. To the south, it met Westbury here on the ridgeway. To
the east, Passage Road; to the north, the railway line; and to the west,
the boundary was completed by the woods and parklands of Blaise
Castle Estate.

Henbury's road system was simple. Henbury Road joined Hallen
Road after a double bend in the centre to roughly bisect the village.
Station Road left Henbury Road just before the shops, to run north east

27

to the railway station and Cribbs Causeway. Kings Weston Road led from the junction of Henbury and Hallen Roads through countryside to the village of Lawrence Weston. Crow Lane was a farm lane leading from the ford to Passage Road and the Old Crow Inn.

Ray knew the stream well as it ran along the edge of grandfather's farm to ford Henbury Road by the show ground. There was a road bridge as well as the ford. From here, a lane led up to the church of St Mary, the Vicarage and Henbury Awdelett.

There were so many places and people to renew acquaintance with! But he checked himself: 'I'm no longer a boy on holiday, but a farmer come to prove my worth.'

Through the haze, an impression of green was everywhere insistent. The lushness of the Royals was contained by a handsome grey stone wall. Opposite, on the right, cows grazed The Elms pasture safely behind hedge and ditch. He thought he could see Robert and John playing in their garden, but they were small boys and would not remember him, he was sure.

A terrible bellowing from behind reminded him that William Budgett of Tramore kept a fierce bull for servicing his Jersey cows, the calves of which he traded round the world.

He passed Henbury House, Endcliffe, the Salutation (of fond memories), briefly glanced at the trim Georgian terrace near the corner, had a good stare at Fane Cottage but did not see Great Aunt Annie. He turned the horse into Crow Lane and soon pulled up at the gates of Westmoreland Farm . . . and there was Aunt Dorothy in the yard talking to the carter. Suddenly seeing him, she called, 'Come along in Ray, tea is ready. I'm so glad to see you.'

Planning the future

The days and weeks sped by. The young farmer was familiarising himself with the farm routine. More than that, he was planning, and it turned out that his plans fairly coincided with those of his Aunt Dorothy. She had everything to gain by remaining in her home among her friends.

By this time, her stepmother had taken herself back to her own house. The will had declared that all stock and equipment were to be sold and the proceeds invested. The widow was to enjoy a life-time claim to the interest. At her death, the capital would revert to William's children. Mr Charles Newman of Raglan Villa, who acted in various official capacities, including Clerk to Henbury Police Court was processing the necessary documentation.

Dorothy had saved from the wages her father paid her for her housekeeping duties. Ray had saved money from enterprises carried out on his father's farm; and an uncle offered to help, also. With this small combined fortune in the bank, and plans agreed, they spoke to William George. He approved and agreed to stand surety with the bank for necessary loans.

The day shortly arrived when Ray and his father went to see Major Sampson-Way. They came away with his agreement to a twelve-month probationary tenancy for Ray provided he paid the three farmworkers and the rent, rates etc for the farm. It was a sobering outcome for William George, but for his young son, it was a resounding triumph. Surely it was a case of 'Where ignorance is bliss, 'tis folly to be wise'?

March 27th 1931, the sale day, arrived with the auctioneers and their itemised lists. Farmers came from a fair distance around, looking for bargains. Other people came out of idle curiosity or just to enjoy a 'day out', for light refreshments were served. In spite of hard bargaining, there was also a festive air about these occasions. Dorothy and Ray had noted items they had decided to bid for and were likely to be able to afford . . . and the Sale began.

The young man who rode into Henbury so optimistically, convinced that here lay his life's work ahead of him, was to keep doggedly on, gaining experience from his mistakes, maturing through adversity and achieving some quite outstanding successes. At the peak of success in the prime of his life, he had to learn to face disaster from circumstances beyond his control. The following chapters follow and describe his career, so closely welded to the final years of Henbury's farming history.

3 – 'Blissful ignorance'

Horses

This story contains frequent mention of horses. In Henbury, like most other villages before the war, horses were only slowly giving way to the combustion engine. So, in 1930, horses still pulled the ploughshare and everything else in and around the farm as well as off it. The milk round, bread and coal deliveries, goods to market and shops – all were pulled by horses. At that time, the only public transport servicing Henbury was a two-hourly country bus travelling between Westbury on Trym and New Passage – afternoons only! People used their feet, bicycles or horseback to get about. Cars were owned by some of the better-off families. In many respects people were living in a similar fashion to their parents and grandparents.

Conditions of the tenancy

The new farmer describes his early years:

'Now, in accordance with the terms of my tenancy, I had to pay £320 per annum rent, plus rates, water, phone and services – another £60. I also had to keep on the three farmworkers.

'There was a carter named Rugman, a cowman named Lukins and a younger, single man, Bill Willie, a general labourer. Rugman and Lukins lived with their families in two semi-detached cottages at Dragonswell. They were paid 29 shillings and sixpence per week, and in addition, they received a pint of milk a day, cider, and gleanings from the threshing and the fields. They were also allowed a row of cabbages, potatoes and swedes. For this, they started work at 6 a.m. and worked until 6 p.m. Some time later, this was reduced to 5.30 p.m. They had half a day off on Saturday or Sunday. [These were agreed agricultural conditions at the time.]

Basic stock and equipment to start

'My aunt kept house and looked after the poultry. Together, we started with five cows in milk, six yearling heifers, two horses, one sow in pig, twenty five hens, six ducks, one farm cart, two four-wheel wagons, farm machinery and utensils, harness for the horses and general farm tools. We also had a bull cart for transporting cattle to market, which was often borrowed by other local farmers.

The first year

'That first summer, we made fifty tons of hay, about half of which was sold to bring in cash for buying extra milking cows. We ploughed up, for cash also, eight acres using, of course, the horse-drawn plough. The location was opposite Wyck House by the railway station. We then put in three acres of mangolds and swedes, about a half-acre of Savoy cabbage, half-acre of sprouts and the rest in mixed vegetables – turnips, cauliflowers and broccoli (for winter).

'Using a horse-drawn crank-axle cart, I took the vegetables into Westbury on Trym and elsewhere. My first customer was Mrs Filer whose son kept a saddler's shop (a lock-up, I think) at the bottom of Westbury hill. Mrs Filer sold her vegetables outside the front of the shop. [The site is now occupied partly by the new Foresters Arms and Barclays Bank] Later, the Filers moved their saddler's shop into their house, the tall Georgian house opposite, and the greengrocery into a small lean-to at the hill side of the house. This brought Mrs Filer next door to Clake the baker. On that first visit to Mrs Filer, she bought one or two hundredweights of potatoes and a dozen or so Savoys and cauliflowers.

'I took the horse and cart round on Tuesdays and Thursdays and built up a clientèle who gave me fairly consistent regular orders. These customers included Leach of Henleaze who owned seven shops this side of Bristol: Coldharbour Road, two on Blackboy Hill, Clifton Down, Chandos Road and others. I went in search of business orders either on bike or on horseback. On delivery days, I built up the cart with loose vegetables on top of sacks of potatoes and roots and bags of sprouts. They were stacked 'scientifically', mind you and 'artistically', no boxes – just produce – a sight to behold!

Time passed

'By now, seventy five to one hundred chickens and hens, as well as large quantities of geese, ducks and turkeys ran round the yard loose, or as we say today, 'free range'. The hens often made their nests and laid their eggs in the hay racks or in the mangers of the stable, but the horses did not interfere with them or damage them at all. The chickens and eggs we sold locally to villagers and other private customers. Approaching Christmas time we would bring on cockerels and geese and take orders for the Christmas tables of the locals. For such occasions, we employed

Farmer Ray with mower.

A calf emerges.

'Free-range' geese.

Potato harvesting at Top Field. A two-winged plough is being used to dig the vegetables.

Ordinary winged plough as used throughout the rotation. (print from Rural History Centre, University of Reading)

Crank axle cattle cart: 'bull cart' as used by Farmer Ray to transport cattle to market.

A later version of this type was used to carry vegetables to Westbury-on-Trym, Clifton and elsewhere. (both prints from Rural History Centre, University of Reading)

four or five women to hand-pluck the poultry.'

Apples

Six acres of orchard were inherited from William. Farmer Ray and his workers would pick all the culinary fruit and sell it direct to the shops. The remainder was stamped down and stored for cider-making. There were also lots of Morgan Sweets, a variety of apple that was sold by the tree to local merchants who came themselves to hand-pick the fruit and send it to the dye-works, Brooks. From the fruit they extracted a fast dye of a browny-blue colour.

Dairy and bakery

In grandfather William's time, butter and cheese were made in the dairy behind the house, some for sale and some for home-consumption. In Ray's time, he and his aunt made it only for their own use. Similarly, in William's day, bread was made in the farm bakery, but Ray and his aunt dropped this custom. Instead they got their bread from a baker who kept a small farm with a few cows right on the banks of the Severn. He baked quartern loaves and delivered the bread in a 'cobern', a covered cart, twice a week.

'Cobern' used for bread delivery.

Looking ahead

Each year, profits were put back into the farm and they increased stock and arable. Ray had passed his trial period of twelve months and looked forward with some confidence. The bank overdraft went up but bank inspectors were satisfied that the farm assets provided good surety for the loan. In the nature of farming as well as other commercial and industrial enterprises, profits lag outlay, sometimes worryingly. Sometimes it is money owed to the business, more often in farming it is the season or the weather. In spite of this, they made steady progress.

The end of the first five years

By then they owned twenty five cows, twenty young cattle and calves, twenty five breeding ewes. Ray was asked if he sheared his own sheep. The answer was 'Yes, and other farmers' sheep, too!' He continued: 'It was very hard work before electric shears came in, not only for the shearer but for the poor soul turning the handle of the mechanical clippers (a bit like the barber's clippers). In earlier times again, hand shears were used.

'The ewes ran on the fields after the cattle, cattle grazing the fields loose and sheep grazing tighter – for a better grass-face.

'We had also six or seven sows for breeding; they farrowed twice a year, the piglets would then be sold on. Aunt Doll continued to keep the fowls in order, and she fed them and all of us hungry workers. In all our efforts, the farm workers were indispensable, of course.

'The farm operated a four-course rotation: autumn ploughing, then cross plough in early winter and again in spring (this would break up the turf), then harrow. Root crop; beans or oats; potatoes, swedes and mangolds; then wheat and when three inches high, in March/April, undersow with red clover and rye.'

Keeping in touch

Life on a farm can be isolated especially whilst building the business up to maximum efficiency. The McEwen Smiths had many business contacts, and the nearby village shops were useful and friendly. The shops they used most were the smithy, the cobbler and the Post Office. The first two were highly necessary as shoes, both horse and human, get heavy wear in farming work. The Post Office and Miss Stevens kept them in touch with business and the outside world most efficiently.

Two difficult encounters

Two rather tricky encounters serve as a reminder that this was a very young man doing a mature man's job. The first was when he had occasion to get to know Sgt. Harding of Henbury Police Station rather too well. He had just bought a second-hand motor bike for £5, and was caught riding it on the road without tax. In Farmer Ray's own words, 'I was riding with two of my younger employees and a basket of cabbage plants on their backs to take to Wyck Field. I usually drove across the fields but this day, I decided to go round the road where we came upon Sgt. Harding and were not quite quick enough turning round and getting away! The magistrates who fined me ten shillings were Mrs. Budgett of Tramore and my landlord, Major Sampson-Way. It was my first and last appearance in Henbury Police Court!'

Another rather worrying experience was with a group of Master butchers. He learnt many lessons in his youthful farming, mostly from bitter experience. The lessons not only related to husbandry skills; in fact, he believes most of them related to the business side of farming and trying to cope with human nature – his own and others!

Now, in those pre-war days, butchers had their own slaughter-houses at the back of their shops, hence the name 'butcher'. These premises had to be inspected and licenced. Butchers who were licenced were known as 'Master' butchers. Those who did not slaughter, but just cut up and jointed were known as 'jointers'. In about 1936/37, Ray became licenced to slaughter calves, sheep and pigs. An inspector had to come after the slaughter and cutting up and before he could sell. He explains why he decided to do his own slaughtering:

'I was beginning to lose money on sale of stock at auction due to an iniquitous practice of price-rigging. Dealers and butchers would pre-arrange together each to bid for different stock on any given day, just one would bid for sheep, another for pigs etc., so that they were not competing with each other. Later, they would sell to each other at the low prices they had achieved. The unhappy farmer was then forced to choose between an unrealistic offer or buying back his own stock as well as paying the auctioneer's fee!

'A group of local butchers had formed a 'ring' against me, and I had to take avoiding action by becoming licenced. However, this alarmed the local 'ring' as I was successfully selling directly to customers. They next formed a deputation to discuss the situation with me. We at last came to an agreement. I would cease slaughtering provided the three of them arrived at my farm every Monday morning and bought everything I had on offer – at a fair market price. Being an enterprising young fellow, if I fell short in any week, I bought up round the farms and included this

Down on the farm.

Mother and child.

as part of the deal.'

Local business contacts

There was little social contact between farmers and villagers on the one hand and residents of the big houses on the other. However, there was a small amount of business contact for Farmer Ray. He took the horse-drawn cutter to cut the grass for the Budgett family at Tramore, and also sometimes supplied Mr Sommerville Gunn of Henbury House with hay and straw for his horses. Another job was to cut the grass and make hay for Mr Charles Farr at Brentry Lodge. Yet another enterprise was to supply the Lord Mayor's Mansion House stables with hay and straw – and pick up the manure for use on his farm.

The village gets together

There was, though, one notable exception to the social separation of the 'classes'. Ray remembers that 'when the lily pond froze hard, all, from rich to poor joined in the fun. The Sampson-Way family, who had created the pond, would bring a carriageful of visitors. It was a large spectacular pond full of waterlilies and fish.'

Aptly, it seems the swimming pool was, years later, built right in front of it. But that was long after the pond had dried out and the lilies and fish had been carried off to many small private ponds. For, with the death of the Major and the changes that followed, life was never the same again. But all this was, in the mid-1930s, still in the future.

In summertime, Lily Pond Field was covered with mushrooms, and early-morning pickers and gatherers could be seen filling their baskets in anticipation of a bacon and mushroom breakfast! The cows happily grazed around the pond nearly all year round. One can see on the map just where the lily pond was, and how close to Westmoreland Farmhouse.

Beginning of change

In the mid-thirties, many changes were taking place. To start with, Henbury ceased to be part of Gloucestershire and joined the City and County of Bristol. Not that Henbury villagers noticed any difference for they still considered themselves a Gloucestershire village for many years after 1935. Much more noticeable changes were happening to the land round the edges of Henbury. Farmland between Westbury and Henbury and between Westbury and Stoke Bishop was fast disappearing as developers carried out vast house-building schemes.

40

Traffic from Bristol to New Passage and Gloucester could now bypass the centres of Westbury and Henbury via the new Falcondale Road and the widened Passage Road. New houses were going up along Passage Road, and there were changes round Wyck House. In Wyck Beck Road now were Brent Breck, Tylsdale, The Cabin, Cradley and Arden. Passage Road was rerouted in this area too. The motor car was becoming more in evidence and consequently roads were busier. There was increased traffic through Henbury, too, when summer visitors started to come to Blaise Castle Estate for family outings.

There were a few changes in house ownership, several in Wyck Beck Road. St Brendan's Preparatory Day School came to Henbury Hill House, there were changes at Chesterfield House and Endcliffe. Wilfred Ironside was the new manager of the new Salutation Inn. There was a new district nurse, Mrs England. At Station Yard, coal merchant Dowding gave place to Brown and Goodfield. North Lodge, the Dower House, the Chalet and Chevening House changed hands. Even in a tiny village, there is inevitable gradual change as old people die and others seek work elsewhere.

The thirties draw to a close and the use of horses declines further

And now that at last combustion engines were beginning to get into everything – the motor car, farm machinery, public transport – the smiths had to change direction. They continued to repair metal implements and turned more to making metal artefacts as horse-shoeing went into sharp decline. Jimmy Grigg eventually gave up his smithy. At about seventy, he was probably ready to retire and his son, also Jimmy, was by now well-established in his own smithy in Westbury.

In spite of all this movement and activity and increased traffic noise, the appearance of Henbury Village, its population numbers and land-use had scarcely changed since Ray's early childhood, and probably his grandfather's childhood, too.

In the following chapter, Farmer Ray describes the seasonal round on his farm, typical of farming in those days.

4 – Cycle of the year

In managing a farm, all well-laid plans must take into account, above all else, the unpredictability of our climate – no good ranting against it, just go with it! One eye and ear should be on the weather, and the plan must always include contingencies.

Hay-making

So let us start talking about June . . . the hay-making process commences early June and continues to about the end of July. This involves mowing, turning and drying, then gathering and rick-making; and finally thatching the rick with corn-stalks. In the early days, hand rakes were used for turning over the swathes of mown grass; later, a swathing machine was used but, even then, heavy areas such as clover still needed a hand-rake. The mown grass would then be left for twenty four hours or more to dry before collection by horse-drawn wagon.

Carting home

Some of the hay was then carted home to the farm and stored in hay barns for the cows which were kept in sheds in the winter. On one such 'carting home' occasion we had a near catastrophe. It happened like this: Crow Lane was narrow and muddy running between high banks and hedges. Not a building was to be seen between our farm and the Old Crow Inn. I was leading Shire horses pulling a wagon loaded with hay along the lane. Carter Rugman was sitting on top, keeping the hay steady. A wagon wheel caught on a clod or stone, the cart tipped, Tom and hay landed in an undignified heap in the ditch! Happily, Tom lived to tell the tale.

Rick-building

The rest of the hay was put into ricks for feeding out to cattle in the fields during winter. Ricks were based on a foundation of hedge trimmings, dry docks, nettles and such like to keep the hay up off the ground. Even so, when the rick had settled, the roof would sink and rain would get in and spoil a lot of the hay. We used to rock and pull all four sides of the rick into good shape, and use the pullings to top up and make good the roof ready for thatching.

Rick thatching

Now, to thatch a rick we used sheaves of wheat straw and spars which we made from withy trees in winter spare times. The wheat straw was damped and leazed [stripped] to clean off loose straw; and you should only use the straight stems for thatching. In winter we would go to the woods or hedges and cut straight hazelnut saplings for bonds on roof of hay or corn ricks when thatching. It must be realised that hay-making needs fine weather so the work had to proceed through June and July during dry sessions, with other jobs done on wet days.

A typical day

During these months, work for all of us started at 4 a.m. when it was still dark and chill, in order to mow while the dew was still on the grass. Preparation for mowing meant getting out horses, grooming horses, arranging harness, getting out the mowing machine and linking horses to mower. Between 5 a.m. and 7 a.m., cows had to be milked, the milk had to be cooled and made ready for the churns and the milkman, Hignell.

The business side of milking

In 1935, we had installed a three-unit milking machine to be managed by one man; and this was a boost to efficiency. In the days before the Milk Marketing Board agreed a minimum price for farmers' milk, economic arrangements were agreed between a farmer and his milkman. The terms we made were that I was paid an extra $1\frac{1}{2}$d per gallon all year round for an agreed amount of milk, an even, steady supply. This steady supply had to be managed by 'staggering' the calvings; we 'rationed' the bull and 'dried off' the cow three months before calving. Nature dictates more milk per cow during summer months, with fresh green grass to eat and a sense of well-being no doubt the reasons. This would normally mean cheaper milk in the summer and dearer in winter. As my terms stood, the milkman could recoup by selling any surplus to butter and cheese factories. From about 1941, I started to build up a Pedigree attested herd of Friesians, and for this milk, I was able to charge 3d per gallon extra – because of the attestation.

The typical day

To return to a typical day on the farm, breakfast would be taken in the farmhouse kitchen, always warm and always with a kettle on the hob. In the 'cellar' nearby, cider barrels rested, and sides of bacon dried from the rafters (our cellar was on the same level as the kitchen). New-laid eggs and bacon, what breakfasts!

Crops for the animals

When hay-making was stopped by bad weather, other jobs became more pressing. Ploughing and hoeing were ongoing tasks, horses being used to pull plough and hoe. Crops had to be grown for the working animals as well as for human consumption. Mangolds were sown for the cattle about on the first day or two of May, swedes for the cattle about the end of June, and turnips for the sheep in early July. Of course, sheep would graze the fields in the growing season but at the end of December, through January and February, when lambing was in process in the folds, turnips were the sheep's fodder, while they sheltered from the cold and wet under wattled hurdles covered with straw.

Another crop for the cattle was marrow-stemmed kale that grew five feet high! This was sown about May 1st and was later harvested, cut daily and carried to the milking cows. At certain times of the year, I had to keep the milking cows out of Trap-style field because the wild garlic that grew in the hedgerows, if eaten by the cows, would taint the milk.

Back to a typical day

By mid-day everyone was starving hungry again, and the farmer and his men each returned home for the main meal of the day. However, on hay-making days, the women brought tea in glass bottles kept warm in a wrapping, bread and cheese and sandwiches. Milking was done again at 4.30 p.m. – twenty five to thirty cows milked by three people (that was before we bought the milking machine). Bed was usually 11 to 12 p.m., followed by about five hours sleep, provided all was well and quiet with the stock. This typical routine happened seven days every week except for alternate Sundays off on a rota basis. Who would be a farmer? Well, it's my way of life, I know no other!

Corn harvest: reaping and binding

August, and havesting begins – the busiest month of the year. Our corn crops were oats and barley for cattle and family; and wheat, the best of all, to sell. Seconds – screenings – were for the poultry. Harvesting began, using hand scythes to create a ten-foot margin round the field with twenty feet at the corners. This was to allow room for the 2 or 3 horse-drawn reaper and binder to start off. The product of the hand-cutting had, of course, to be bound and tied by hand too.

Stooking

When the entire field was finally reaped and bound, stooking took place. A sheaf would be grasped under each arm and propped upright together, heads up to the bright sky. Five or six such pairs would be propped up together giving mutual support. These would then be left to dry. To test: rub a grain-head – if dry enough, there is no milk. It is then fit to haul into the dutch barn, where it is built into a rick.

To build a corn rick

Start in the middle and work round in a spiral. This ensures that the heads are upright and overlapping. The rick will settle and can be left until the price is right – up to twelve months, but beware of rats and mice and keep many cats. A rick is also useful collateral against the bank loan – all part of the farmer's need to juggle output, overdraft, bad debts, prediction – and keep sane!

Threshing

Now comes the smelly, sweaty part. When the time *is* right and your turn has come for the thresher, and the drum and steam engine are on their way, collect together ten strong men (or women), not forgetting you will need to reciprocate when their turns come. This machine is now largely superseded by the combine harvester that does the whole job out in the field from reaping to trussing and separating the grain; but this does not detract from the usefulness of the threshing machine in its time. Out of one end of the threshing machine issued the trussed and bound stalks, at the other end the heads were blown by fans through shaking sieves of three different-sized holes. You ended up with best quality, seconds, weed seeds and small corn. The chaff was blown out at the side, and straw would be laid down to collect it. Weed seeds were disposed of, because if cattle ate it, the land would be soon overgrown with weeds. Corn and hay were stored in a large 7-bay barn opposite the older part of the house and adjoining Home Field.

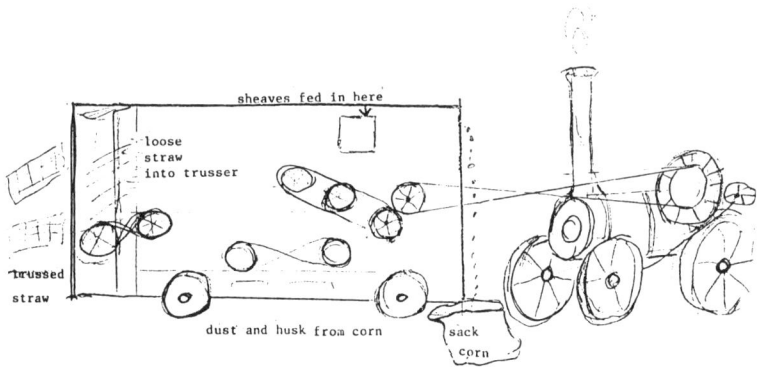

Steam-powered thresher.

Manufacture of winter feed

I must mention winter feed at this point because it is another ongoing job, using chaff, among other ingredients. It is made on the same principle as a 'rum-pot' or 'layer cake'. One may start with a layer of hay or corn chaff, then a layer of roots such as swedes or mangolds (the roots are first put through the pulper, swedes emerging like long fingers, sweet and juicy). Then one puts on a layer of crushed oats, barley or maize. Finally a layer of oily substance is added such as cattle cake, linseed or cotton seed cake (after the oil has been extracted at the mill). When this cake is crushed, it is spread as a top dressing. These layers are built up daily over the autumn and winter until the mound is about eight to ten feet high. Nothing could be nicer for a cow in her winter shed dreaming of green fields than to be given a tasty slice of winter feed cake!

Hens

These are all-important for sale and for family use. At Westmoreland Farm, like its neighbours, hens were free-ranging. We had poultry houses in the orchard at the back of the barn and in the rick yard by the dutch barn, behind Westmoreland Cottage. The poultry houses were wooden with galvanised roofs; and they had to be cleaned every week and disinfected with Jeyes Fluid.

Apple harvest

There was a small orchard behind the farmhouse that is nowadays grass lawn and borders, and kitchen garden. But the main orchard of six acres – about fifty trees – was along the river bank by Furlongs

46

(Trapstyle Field). About September and October was apple harvest time. The best were picked by hand and stored on straw to mature for the Christmas trade, especially the cookers. Some were used for family as well as for sale. The 'seconds' were used for making cider.

Apples for cider

Apples were beaten on the ground with sticks until the orchards were carpeted with the broken fruit and the air hung thick with the scent. Sacks were then filled and loaded onto corn wagons. Then they were stored and left until the end of October, early November. They were then taken out and ground into a pulp between stone rollers and the crushed pulp collected into long troughs.

Pressing the apple pulp

Next, the pulp was put into a press in this way. It was placed in the centre of a horsehair cloth (later on, coconut fibre was used) and the cloth folded in and over until the dimensions were about four feet square. These squares were placed one on top of another on to the base of the press, until it was full. The screws were then turned evenly, finally using a pole through the handles for extra leverage. Turning of the screws had to be done every two or three hours. At last, it was left overnight while the liquid ran along the runnels and into a stone trough.

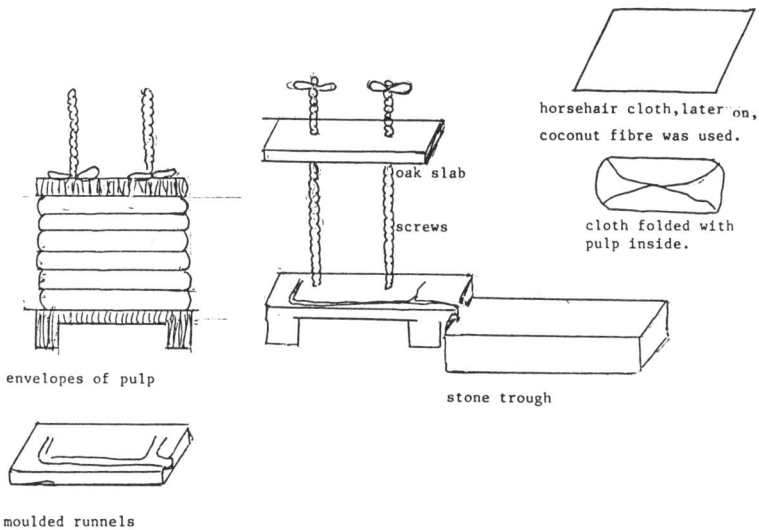

Apple press for making cider.

47

Fermentation

The liquid from the trough was poured into barrels with the top bung open. Fermentation went on in the barrels' frothing-out process. Each day, the liquor reduced four to five inches. The barrels were kept topped up for one week; when frothing stopped, fermentation was complete. The barrels were finally levelled to the top to exclude the air and the bungs tightly inserted.

The gravity

After three or four months the cider was mild; after twelve months pretty strong. If you wanted to add to the gravity, you siphoned liquor to another barrel and added about ten pounds of sugar. The process of fermentation and topping up proceeded as above. After two or three months a much stronger cider was achieved. The pulp remaining in the press could be broken up again and added to other once-used pulp, water added and the press recharged. One ton of apples made one hundred gallons of cider. The cider – about eight to ten barrels – was then stored in cellar, byre and barn.

Enhancing the cider

The barrels that we used were bought from liquor importers. A hogshead of 90 gallons capacity had shipped spirits – whisky, rum or gin – to this country. The pipe, capacity 120 gallons, had shipped port wine. As you may well imagine, the aroma and 'presence' of these spirits and wines were an enhancement to the cider within! When this influence had worn away with time and usage, a bottle of gin tipped into a barrel of cider did much to recapture the memory. Some of the cider was set aside for the farmworkers during haymaking, and the rest was sold, about 400 to 500 gallons.

Then came winter

Cattle wintered in cowsheds this side of the hay barn and back of the cottage. Chores at this time of year were quite a trial. Pigs, poultry and cow houses had to be cleaned out twice each day. The water tank was in the yard, and there was no running water. A few cows were loosed at a time to drink and exercise. The men had then to get in, tie up the rest and so on. Manure was wheeled out and put in huge stacks until, in February, it was hauled in carts and spread over the fields. Then the cleaning was undertaken, cows put back, more taken out and so on.

The cows were fed hay twice a day, and watered. Hay was cut into chaff for the feed; it was cut from a rick with hay-knives, and carried on heads to the cowbarn. Some of this was used for the chaff/feed mixture; and this mixture as already described was fed to the cows also twice a day.

Then came the spring again

This was a new start of planting, cultivating, manuring. But some corn was planted in October or November; and the rest in March, April, May. So there was winter corn and spring corn.

It has already been written that Major Sampson-Way placed trust in me, when as a boy of eighteen I asked him for the tenancy of Westmoreland Farm. Each year subsequently, I went to the Major's house, Henbury Awdelett, for the annual rent audit. Here, with the other tenant farmers, I was served a glass of sherry while we waited in turn for our interviews with the Major. We then chatted to him about repairs and such matters. After four years, the rent went up – and kept going up!

The farmer and his dog.

5 – Friends and neighbourhoods

How did a young farmer relax from his heavy responsibilities in those pre-war days? There was no T.V., no computers, no chance of a car to run around in. The 'wireless' was at an early stage. Well, this young farmer managed to enjoy himself hugely with his friends. Here are some of the things they got up to:

'Farming was a hectically busy way of life, but I would not want anyone to think I regretted it. But, as Aunt Doll kept reminding me, "All work and no play makes Jack a dull boy." As the first year passed and the future began to look promising, I started having time out with my friends.

My friends! What a long time ago it was. We drank at the Salutation – the small old country pub that grandfather knew so well. Then later on, we drank at the new one. We had a darts team and some of us joined the skittles team at the White Lion in Westbury.

A few names come to mind – Arthur Harvey, and Tom White of Fishpool Hill. Then there were Arthur Williams, Arthur White, Jim Croker the carpenter, and Richard (Buller) Croker who was milk roundsman to Stan Biggs of The Elms. There was Ray Chapman of Pilning, too. We would go everywhere competing in darts and skittles. We played for Severnside skittles at the King's Arms in Redwick and we even won the cup. In fact, one year we won all three cups – singles, doubles and team!

Special friends in the early days were Arthur Harvey, Tubby Spencer, a commission agent and Chinny Lewis, a local character. Another friend was Stan Biggs of The Elms and Jo Rowles of Charlton Road who farmed at Pen Park. Jo's sister married Stan Biggs.'

Encouragement was given by some of his older new friends, such as George Hignell who had been a friend of his grandfather. George was distantly connected to Clem Hignell of Norton Farm. Ray remembers George when he used to stay at Westmoreland Farm in school holidays. 'George used to rent some of Blaise Castle park to graze his five or six Guernsey cows. I would accompany him on his horse-drawn crank cart with milk churn, two buckets and two milking stools. We would milk the cows out in the park and take home the milk.

In Ray's early days of farming, George arranged to sell 25 gallons of his milk per day from his cows. In this he was helped by his son,

Harry who carried a large can of milk over each handlebar of his bike. He would ladle milk from his can into the customer's jug. This was quite common practice in those days, though usually from a horse-drawn trap rather than from a push-bike. George was also a general farm dealer buying and selling, mostly calves.

Some time later, this same son Harry, with his wife, started a shop in Passage Road. In the shed behind the shop, they bottled up milk, and also sold sweets. In course of time, this grew into a general stores, a thriving business.

From boyhood to manhood

As Farmer Ray reached his later twenties and became a little more mature, his social and leisure life widened out from pub pursuits. His Aunt Dorothy, we believe, was delighted with this. She was very keen on tennis and so, it turned out, was her nephew. They together rediscovered the tennis-court over on Home Field, and ran it as a club. For an annual subscription of £1 per member, they were able to employ a man to cut the grass and mark out the white lines. There were about twenty members and this was enough to keep the club self-supporting. Most were family and close neighbours and friends. The Biggs family were very involved until, some years later, they built their own court.

A 1937 acquisition was a billiard table, kept in the loft over the bakery. Downstairs was used for chicken brooders, about 200 to 300. Ray and his friends attended dances at Westbury Village Hall, Tockington Hall, the Masters Butchers' Dance at the Berkeley, Café, Bristol, as well as dances at Wrington and Nailsea. They still enjoyed a pint at the Salutation, and in Westbury at the White Lion, the Mouse and Post Office Tavern.

Agricultural Shows and Markets

Members of the farming 'fraternity' and business associates met at agricultural shows and over a pint. Henbury had its own show ground where the Hallen and Henbury Show was held annually. It was across the river behind Westmoreland Farmhouse. Most of the time the Major rented it to Stan Biggs for extra grazing.

Other great days out, mixing business with pleasure, were visits to market at Thornbury, Yate, Chipping Sodbury; and in Somerset at Winford; in Bristol, St Nicholas Market. That last one was a fine place years ago. Young farmer Ray says he bought his first gun, a double-barrelled one, from a gun merchant in St Nicholas Street.

Centre of the Village

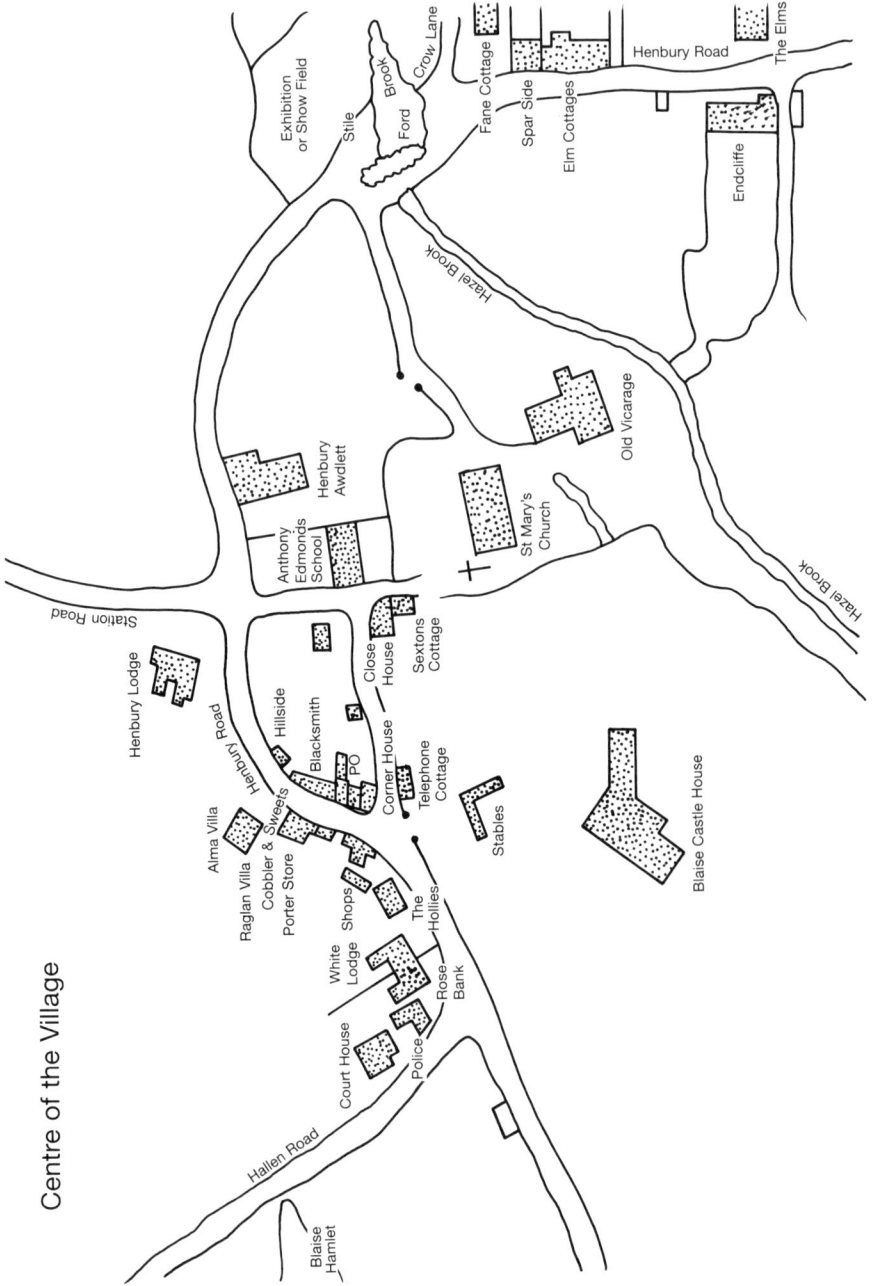

Exhibition or Show Field

Stile

Ford

Brook

Crow Lane

Fane Cottage

Spar Side

Elm Cottages

Henbury Road

The Elms

Endcliffe

Hazel Brook

Old Vicarage

Henbury Awdlett

Anthony Edmonds School

St Mary's Church

Hazel Brook

Station Road

Henbury Lodge

Hillside

Blacksmith

Close House

Sextons Cottage

Henbury Road

Alma Villa

Raglan Villa

Cobbler & Sweets

Porter Store

PO

Corner House

Telephone Cottage

Stables

Blaise Castle House

White Lodge

Shops

The Hollies

Court House

Police

Rose Bank

Hallen Road

Blaise Hamlet

52

Blaise Castle House and Blaise Hamlet

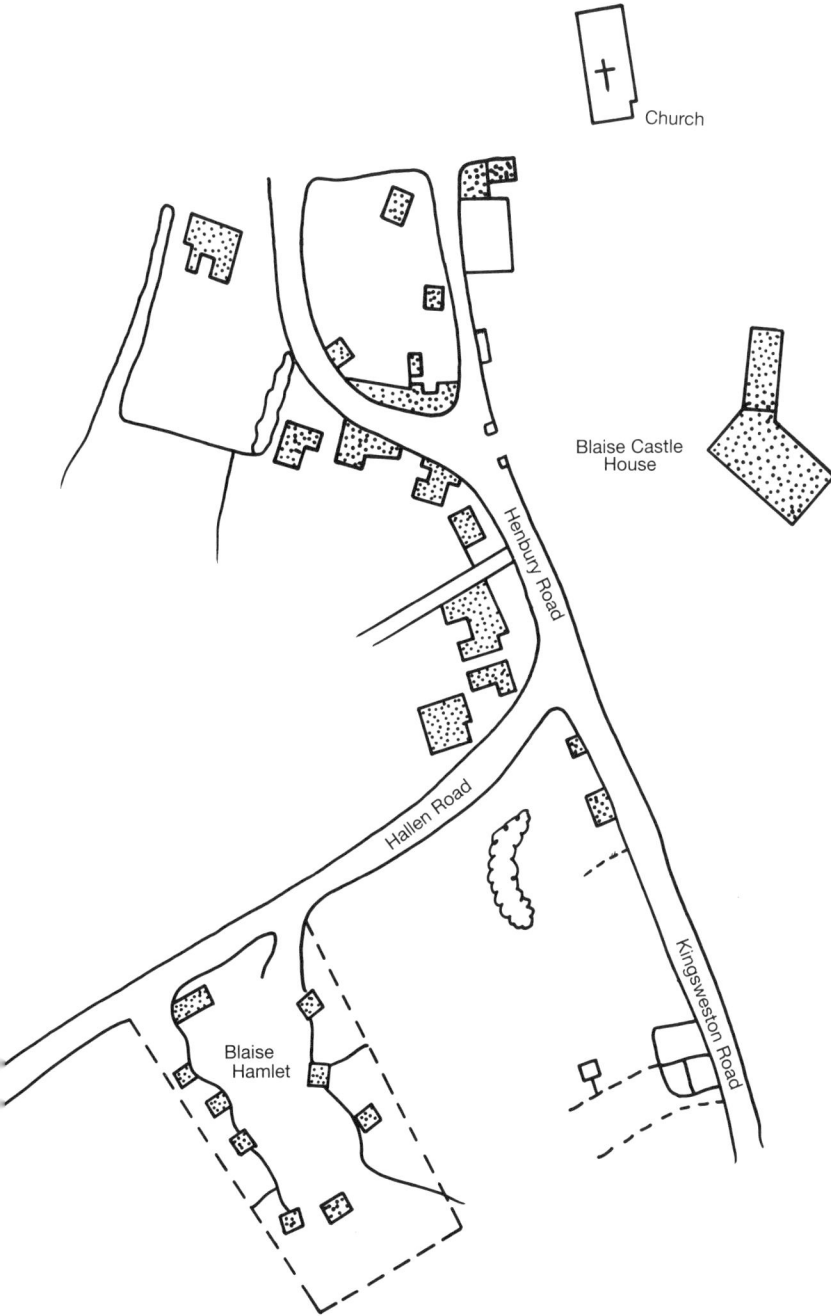

Church

Blaise Castle
House

Henbury Road

Hallen Road

Kingsweston Road

Blaise
Hamlet

Farming friends and neighbours

While the McEwen Smiths were building up Westmoreland Farm, over at Norton Farm, the Hignells – Clem and his wife and their sons, Tom and Bob – were at a well advanced stage with theirs. Their acreage was a third as much again as the Westmoreland Farm acreage. Their land ran next to Ray's across the brook, and stretched away north of the railway line to Haw Wood and east to Brent Knoll along Cribbs Causeway. It stretched west to Ison Hill and the railway 'halt'. In fact, to the east, they were next to the farms of Charlton, the little village that was to be destroyed to build a runway long enough for the Bristol Brabazon.

Also very well-established was the Elms Dairy Farm run by Stan Biggs whose acres reached from his farmhouse on Henbury Road to the Ridgeway, southwards and to Westmoreland on the east. In addition, he grazed his cows on fields next to Blaise Hamlet as well as on the show ground. He was building up a herd of Guernsey cattle and a milk 'round' delivering produce over a large area. He had also a modern, mechanised dairy near his farmhouse.

The following words are not easy to write. However, it seems inappropriate to omit young farmer Ray's closest friends of those days. They were a family called Bendall who farmed at Redhill. He found great happiness with these friends especially when he fell in love with their daughter, Mary and she consented to marry him.

They married and spent a few years farming together. Good Aunt Doll arranged to leave them on their own, and went off to live with an elderly relative to keep house for him.

Happiness did not last, for in the early 1940s, Mary fell ill, and died after a long illness. The prospect for the young husband was bleak. Hard work and yet more hard work became first a great means of escape and then healing. In course of time, farming was the means of bringing him happiness again through a contented family life.

Neighbourhoods

What about the rest of the village? By the late thirties, Ray had become familiar with every corner of it, though he admits he did not know every person who lived there. The map shows that most of Henbury was still grassland, with houses in groups or 'islands' within the 'sea' of green.

Community life between the wars: Mothers' Union and church choir.

Church and Close

The largest and most populated 'island' contains the Parish Church of St Mary. Sunday Services were well-attended. In the week, there was choir practice, Mothers' Union, Communicants' Guild, whist drives and a drama club among other activities. Almost everyone went to church, and it was very much the village social centre too. In the small Vestry by the gates, the Registrar regularly attended to register births and deaths – Mondays between one and two o'clock. Just outside the gates, the Sexton's cottage stood next to the Close House. The Sexton looked after the churchyard, dug graves and rang the bell for services. The Boys' School was opposite Close House. The Anthony Edmonds (Charity) School had been founded in 1624, and Close House had 'boarded' the pupils. But for some years up to the 1930s and '40s, it had been used as a Public Elementary School. So there was always bustle in the Close on Sundays and on weekdays.

Three great houses

Almost equal distances from the church were Blaise Castle House, Henbury Awdelett and the Old Vicarage. By the thirties, Blaise Castle House and Estate were already owned by Bristol Corporation and the woods and park were open to the public. In about 1930, a new vicarage had been built in Station Road and the old building had been purchased by Dr K. Wills. Henbury Awdelett still remained the home of Major Sampson-Way and his family, and would be so throughout the war years.

Village shops and businesses

The shops and houses arranged along the sweep of Henbury Road were very important to the villagers. Starting from Henbury Lodge, then a private house, one came next to Alma and Raglan Villas. Raglan Villa was the home of the Newman family. The father, Charles was first and foremost a schoolmaster at the Boys' School in the Close. He was also, at various times Clerk to Henbury Police Court, tax collector and involved in a number of trusts and charities. He was considered by many to be a 'father confessor' to the village as so many sought his advice and assistance.

The Windsors' sweet and cobbler's shop was attached to the right hand side of the Porter Stores. Years later, when the Porter Stores became Blaise Inn, there were alterations and extensions and the Windsors' shop became the bar-parlour of the renovated building.

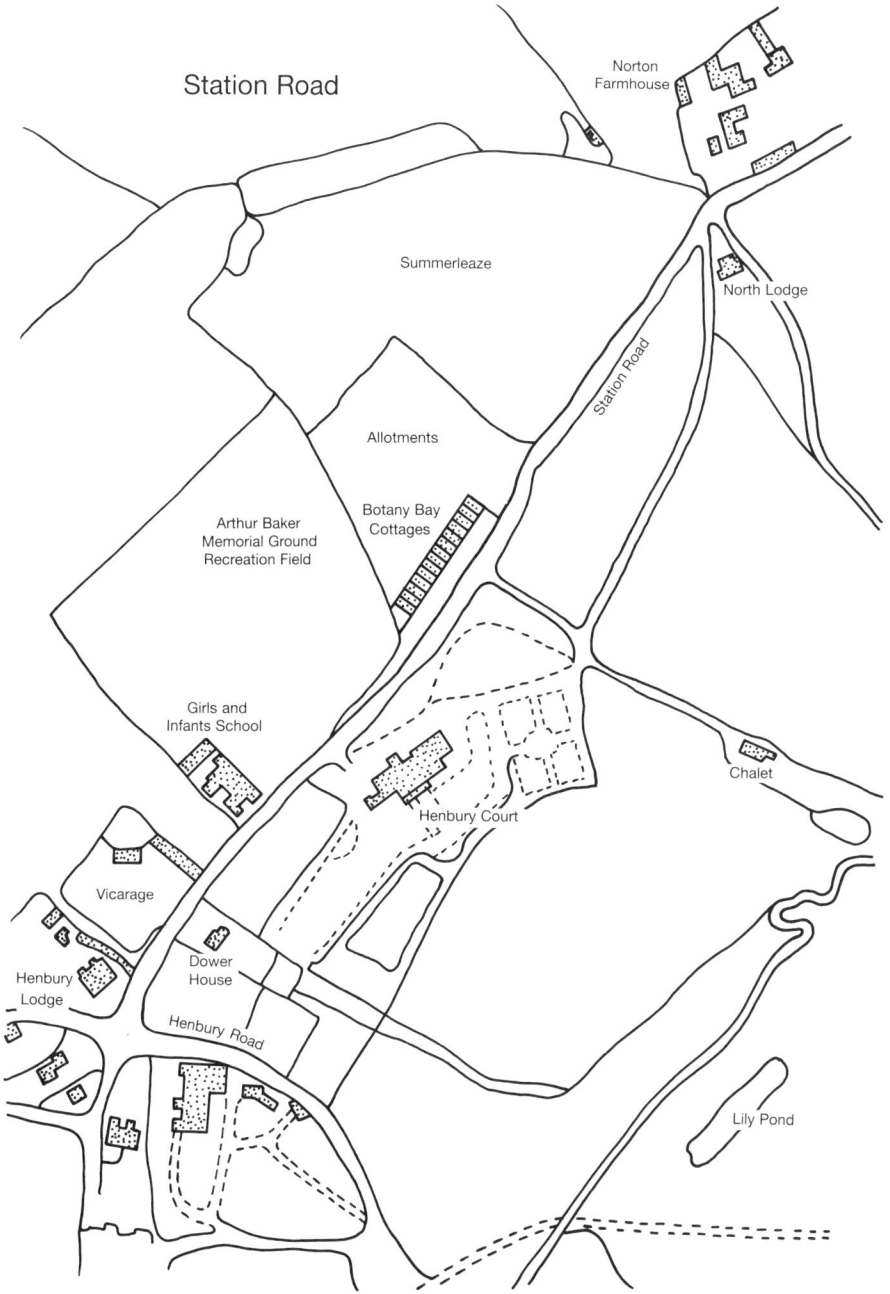

Station Road

Norton Farmhouse

Summerleaze

North Lodge

Station Road

Allotments

Botany Bay Cottages

Arthur Baker
Memorial Ground
Recreation Field

Girls and
Infants School

Chalet

Henbury Court

Vicarage

Dower
House

Henbury
Lodge

Henbury Road

Lily Pond

Next to the Porter Stores, an undertaker, Rossiter had a business partly behind the Porter Stores and the grocer's shop yard. The grocer's shop was mostly used for day-to-day needs as many people had groceries delivered from Westbury. The Henbury grocer was fairly recent because a branch of Westminster Bank had previously used part of the premises. Herbert Harvey's house came next. He was the village plumber and taxi-service.

Three impressive old houses brought one to Hallen Road, the Police Station and Court House, presided over by Sgt. Harding.

Opposite Alma and Raglan Villas was Beaconsfield, a fairly new house and behind it a bungalow, Applegarth. Next to Beaconsfield was a cottage, Hillside, owned by the Major and housing an employee's widow. Then there was the blacksmith's shop, his house, the Post Office and the Corner House. In the lane behind the Post Office was a tiny grey-stone house called Telephone Cottage.

This smattering of shops and businesses was very necessary to a community with little public transport. If one walked into Westbury, one could catch a tram into the City for sixpence and also to suburban areas. The country bus into Westbury was 3d. By the early forties, buses had begun to take over. But it is evident in those pre-war days that church, school, bank, Post Office, shops and services drew people of Henbury into this central area, the heart of the village – a virtually traffic-free zone.

Blaise Hamlet

A short way down the Hallen Road was the small group of cottages called 'Blaise Hamlet' or 'Henbury Cottages'. The cottages, some thatched, were arranged round a 'green' containing a water-pump. The 'hamlet' was built many years ago by the Harfords of Blaise Castle House to house their employees. Because they had the same employer and many had worked together, they knew each other quite well.

Henbury Hill

Another cluster of houses lay between Westmoreland Farmhouse and the summit of the hill. Right on the ridge were Henbury Hill House and Chesterfield House. Tramore, Henbury House and Endcliffe were all large family houses, too. In the 1930s, they employed staffs of servants indoors and chauffeurs and gardeners. Each one was a small 'Upstairs/Downstairs' community.

Between The Elms Farmhouse and Westmoreland Farmhouse was a terrace of small houses – 1 and 2 Elms Cottages and 1 and 2 Sparside

Cottages. These were the family homes of gardeners, farmworkers and a chauffeur. Most of them worked for the local 'gentry' who, in some cases, owned their houses. Mrs Annie Hort lived next to Sparside Cottages at Fane Cottage, a detached house said to be one of the oldest houses in Henbury. She was William McEwen Smith's sister.

Round the corner, in Crow Lane, stood Westmoreland Cottage owned by Major Sampson-Way. In the early thirties, it housed a member of the Major's staff but later reverted to being a farmworker's cottage.

The Salutation comes in this group and provided a centre for much social activity after a heavy day in the fields. Aunt Doll McEwen Smith knew all the neighbours and passed on to her nephew any interesting gossip. Of course, he knew most of it already – through farming business and the 'local'!

Ison Hill

In about the 1920s, Gloucestershire County Council put up a long row of cottages along the road at Ison Hill on the western edge of Norton Farmland. These were very 'modern' houses compared with most of the village housing. A few tenants from Botany Bay moved over there in order to enjoy the 'mod cons' or so one heard tell. The nearest houses to Ison Hill were the great houses of Hill End and Severn House. These were set in large grounds and Hill End had a small home farm.

Station Road

The final 'cluster' was to be found in Station Road. Rather more spread out than the other groups, there were a number of single houses, a hotel, a farmstead and the terraced houses of Botany Bay. Passing Henbury Lodge on the corner, one came to the new vicarage, housing the Reverend John Collins Lloyd and his family. They came to Henbury in about 1930, just after the house was built.

Next door again was the Girls' and Infants' School. A path at the side of the school led to the entrance to the Arthur Baker Memorial Ground, given to the village by Arthur Baker's family in his memory. It was used by, among others, the Henbury and Hallen Football Association. It was also used by the 'Henbury Robins', a boys' team who were later encouraged and helped by Mrs Gunn of Henbury House.

Stretching behind, from Ison Hill to Charlton fields, was Norton farmland. Norton Farmhouse and outbuildings, a community in itself, stood roughly opposite North Lodge.

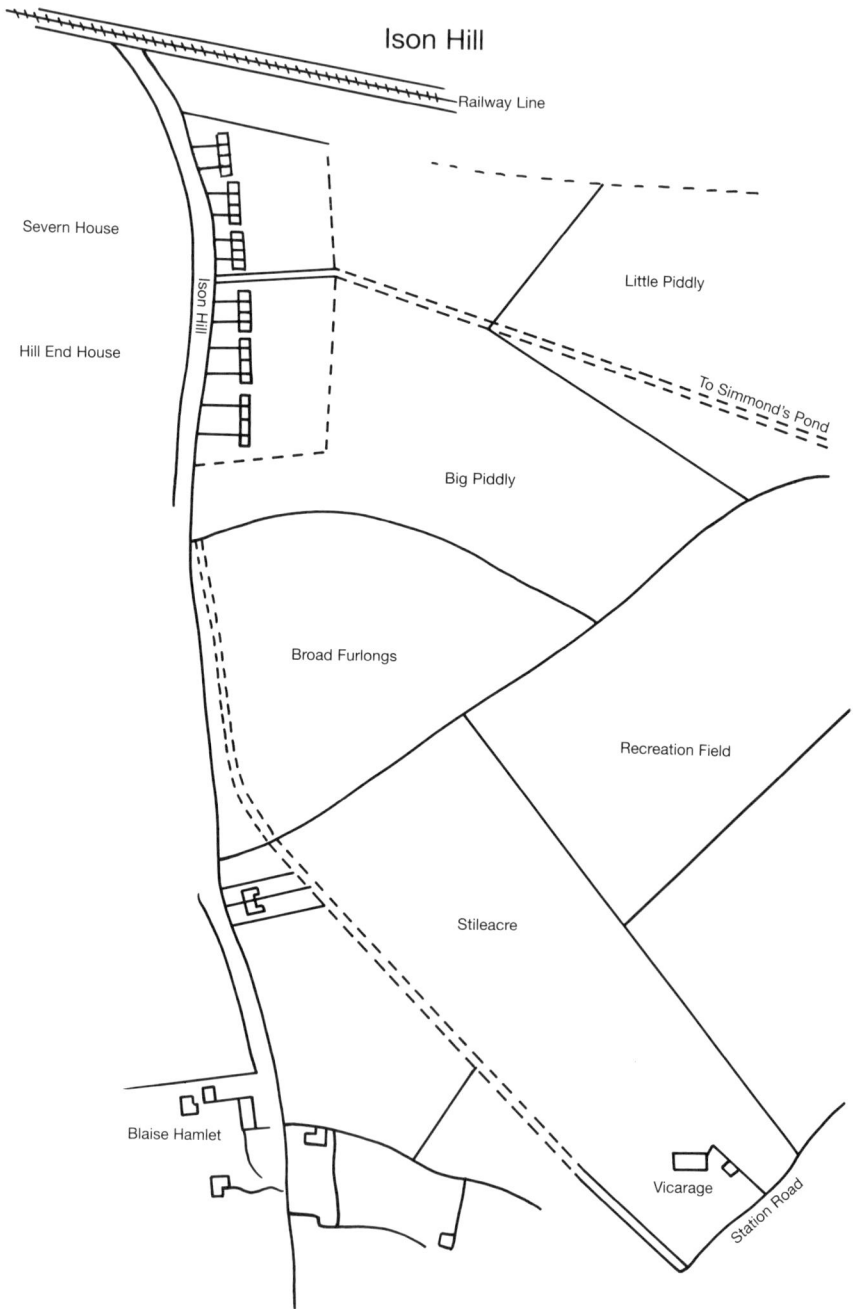

Ison Hill

Railway Line

Severn House

Ison Hill

Little Piddly

Hill End House

To Simmond's Pond

Big Piddly

Broad Furlongs

Recreation Field

Stileacre

Blaise Hamlet

Vicarage

Station Road

60

Botany Bay

Between the school and Norton Farmhouse were Botany Bay cottages, a terrace of fourteen houses built, like Blaise Hamlet, in the early eighteen hundreds and, like the 'hamlet', a small community of friendly neighbours. There, in front of the cottages the children would play with their friends, safely. Traffic was light, one could hear the horses' hooves long before they arrived and there was only an occasional motor car.

Most of the area south and west of North Lodge was taken up by fields, Henbury Court Hotel, the Dower House and Chevening House.

A leisurely progress

Sheep dipping, like many another exercise, was carried out co-operatively between farmers. For a farmer shepherding flocks along road and lanes between Westmoreland and Norton Farms, it was a slow walk and one grew to know the landscape. The formal gardens of Henbury Court and the Dower House made a pleasing contrast with the grazed pasture and neat hedging and ditching with its larger scale of orderliness. The limewash of cottages showed up strikingly the shapes of trees and bushes.

Farmer Ray comments: 'I would lay bets that a modern motorist, driving along Henbury Road to cross the ford between high stone walls, has not experienced a traffic jam to equal a wall-to-wall carpet of woolly sheep on their leisurely return home!'

6 – War-time

By 1938, the threat of war was becoming very real. People turned increasingly from their own preoccupations to listen to the wireless. Neville Chamberlain's appeasement policy bitterly criticised by many since, at least gave the country a much-needed year to prepare for defence.

On September 3rd 1939, the Prime Minister announced that the country was at war. Probably the first noticeable change was the 'black-out'; no chink of light was allowed to show from the outside of any building. Air Raid Wardens were chosen to enforce this, and to co-ordinate rescue and help during raids. Cars had to be driven with much-reduced lighting, street lights were switched off. To add to the confusion, signposts were removed. Church bells were silenced. There was a real fear that the enemy might try to invade, the lack of sign-posts would hinder this and church bells were to be used as a warning that invasion was taking place.

Householders were encouraged to prepare make-shift shelters under stairs or even under heavy tables. Anderson shelters were built in back gardens.

Everyone was issued with an identity card and a ration book. All were issued with gas masks. Children went to school with their masks in cardboard boxes slung round with their satchels. Grown-ups took them to work. Babies had a sleeping-bag type of mask, no one knew what awful possibilities might lie ahead. So began six years of uncertainty, anxiety and sometimes fear.

Young men and women from Henbury, as from other villages and towns, joined the armed services. Yet other young servicemen and women came into Henbury. Behind Westmoreland Farmhouse, across the stream, the Army set up an anti-aircraft gun emplacement. On the Arthur Baker Memorial Ground, there was a Searchlight Brigade whose personnel were housed at Henbury Court Hotel. Later in the war British soldiers were replaced by United States soldiers. Mrs Gunn of Henbury House turned her house into an A.T.S. base and a convalescent home for service people. She also used a small cottage or bakehouse in her garden as a service canteen. The village was probably never so densely populated.

Now, imagine a moonless night, almost total darkness and near silence. Into the strange peace would intrude from time to time the sound of an army truck driving slowly, lowing of cattle, and the low droning of aircraft. Suddenly, a piercing searchlight would illuminate the clouds, followed rapidly by a sharp crack of an anti-aircraft gun repeatedly shooting tracers into the focus of the lights. Soon after, would come whistles and thuds and mighty explosions as Bristol was strafed by enemy aircraft.

This was the background to the war-effort of Henbury, farming village. Farmer Ray recalls the early days of war. 'By the time war broke out, the farm was busy and at full-stretch. Any land unsuited to current needs was rented out for grazing. This was also government policy – no land was to be wasted and must be used to maximum efficiency. The country had to be as self-sufficient as possible.

'For this purpose, public parkland was ploughed up under government contract. I myself worked on many areas as well as on my own farm, sometimes as far as the Downs. Farming in Britain came gradually to be appreciated and the farmer was looked on with some respect as he became an essential factor in the war effort.

'Another example of the government's efficiency drive was recycling of food waste. In towns, local authorities issued pig bins to householder. The contents were collected and used on the farms. The army camps near my farm also produced a lot of food waste – lots of it. I put on a lorry to collect this from the camps and nearby hotels.

'To process all this, we installed a steam-powered cooking plant and cooked a ton of pig-food at a time to feed about three hundred pigs, all shapes and sizes! We had the large boiler in our engine house. When it was boiled up, whey was added to the mixture. This made palatable feeding for the fatting pigs and a dozen breeding sows. It turned out to be highly successful and we won contracts to supply bacon pigs to Harris of Calne in Wiltshire and Spear Brothers in Bristol.'

War brought tragedies and pain. It also brought relief in the quiet times. Life and work had to go on, though there were many occasions when people felt they were fighting for survival. The country was up against a ruthless enemy. As more and more young people offered themselves for the armed services. Farmer Ray decided that he should enlist with the R.A.F. After much thought and heart-searching, he was eventually persuaded that his proven ability to produce food was essential war-work. Training as a fighter pilot takes time and different skills. The cynics said he would most likely end up organising the R.A.F. gardening schemes!

As war proceeded, it became increasingly necessary to plough up every available piece of land. People turned their grass and flower plots into vegetable patches. More parkland was taken over, allotments were

'Tub' outfit: Farmer Ray and 'Cinderella'.

Pigs were a useful meat source in wartime.
Feeding the calves with gruel.

extended. 'Dig for victory!' was the cry up the length and breadth of the land. Anywhere that would yield a food crop was pressed into use.

Under another government contract, Farmer Ray ploughed forty acres of his pastureland to grow some corn. For this he badly needed a tractor. In early 1941, the cattle-feed mills at Avonmouth were bombed. On a journey over there to replenish stocks, he heard they were selling up, and had a tractor for sale. The only snag – it was in Essex! It took 36 hours through snow, ice and pitch darkness to get the cattle-truck there and back and load on the reluctant old tractor. A wonderful all-night roadside café fed them bacon, eggs, sausages – and saved their sanity.

Food had to be home-produced in order to save lives. Ships carrying cargo from overseas were incessantly bombed. War ships accompanied the merchant vessels in 'convoy', but there was still enormous loss of seamen's lives. In normal times the food we ate came from all over the world, but we now had to grow it ourselves. British farmers stepped up their efforts even more, and many, like Farmer Ray, bought another tractor.

And then the farm labourers were 'called up'. They were deemed by the government to be 'dispensable' but not by the farmers who wondered how they would manage without them. For a time at Westmoreland Farm, men from Brentry Colony were employed for an arranged wage, to help out.

And next came the land girls. 'Have they been trained?', asked farmer Ray. 'No', was the reply. So he had to train them and was amazed how dedicated and hard-working they were.

And after that came the 'fireworks'. Ray recollects: 'War-time farming was not at all smooth running. There were the usual disturbances such as losing sleep to tend to cows calving and sows farrowing at inconvenient times. And one got used to spending much of the night in a cold byre instead of a warm bed, but on top of it all were the war-time fireworks! These came in the form of incendiary bombs and parachuted lanterns. Some started fires in hayricks, barns and pigsties. I remember the night Mrs Biggs's henhouse was set alight and all her hens perished.'

Often, the skies were bright with searchlights that lit up the tracers from the emplacement behind the farmhouse. Filton aerodrome was near and, indeed, suffered badly from air attacks, especially early in the war, when extensive damage was done and lives lost.

Avonmouth, with its docks and refineries, was about the same distance away further north west; and Bristol itself was a regular target.

Henbury was virtually at the centre of these vulnerable areas. Villagers and suburbanites alike suffered a share of the attacks. On Westmoreland Farm, sixteen bombs were dropped on various parts of the land; cattle were fatally injured, buildings and house were damaged. Many villagers took night duty as Air Raid Wardens; Ray's duty was in the centre of the village.

But to return to the land-girls, Ray relates, 'There were four or five land girls in all, most were fairly local girls who were not members of the Women's Land Army. They came to do a job and to help with the war effort in producing home-grown food.

'Land girls being a new experience in my life, they became a never-ending source of amusement tinged with terror. Luckily, at the time, I didn't know it, but it was common practice, apparently, after a hard, hot day's haymaking to have a quick strip off and plunge in the river at Pool Leaze.'

Even in war-time, or perhaps especially in times of war, romance flourishes. Into the hectic farming life of Westmoreland Farm came another land girl, this time a member of the Women's Land Army. She was petite and yet strong and had been involved in the world of 'health and beauty' before the war. Since then, she had been through nursing training at Hampstead General Hospital, near her family home in London, when she decided to join the Land Army.

Some years after this, when Farmer Ray's long grieving for his young wife had lost its sharp edge, this attractive land girl, Vivienne became very special to him. Before the war ended, they were married.

Young Vivienne was accident-prone and it was probably the constant amusement she caused that contributed to her attraction. Anyway she made him laugh! Ray says, 'Viv caused me some hair-raising moments! In July 1941, she took the swarth-turner and one of the Shires, called Flower, to Wyck Field. I set her off on the machine and left her to get on with the job.'

Viv takes up her own story: 'Shortly after I started the job, a train in Henbury Station shunted, the horse bolted and I was thrown (mercifully clear of the machine). Nobody had noted the fact that, being a small person, my feet did not reach the footrest – and so I had small "holding" capacity.'

On another occasion, she was turning out a recently calved cow and its calf into Lily Pond field. The farm dog had 'sneaked' behind the cow, who, seeing him, to protect her calf charged, missed the dog and ended up tossing the landgirl into the hedge! Viv says, 'I suffered quite a few bruises and horn marks. Student doctors at Southmead Hospital "hooted" when told how the patient had received her injuries.'

Ray contributed another 'gem'. 'I gave her the nice quiet job of feeding the calves with gruel. Admittedly this was her first attempt, but she couldn't even get this right. By the time she had reached the pen with the warm food and opened the gate, she was charged by the six hungry youngsters. The yoke was knocked off her shoulders and the buckets spilt. She was left sitting in the slops while six busy tongues lapped around her.'

Vivienne wondered what she had let herself in for. Now they were in a reminiscent mood for the funny side of farming, Ray, glancing from a window overlooking the courtyard, was reminded of Policeman Parry, a farmer's son coming across the yard and into the cellar (by invitation of course). He sampled the delectable home-pressed cider, then left *very* happily with six new-laid eggs under his helmet.

This story was finally capped by Vivienne. 'Do you remember our notice "beware of the bull"? In the yard across from the farmhouse, we used to have the farm building electric meter. The chappie reading it one day, heard heavy breathing and turned round to see Ferdinand, our gentle bull, gazing down at him – talk about the 4-minute mile! He was over the road and at the farmhouse door like lightning. We calmed him down and assured him the bull was harmless. However, from then on, anyone reading the meter would see, marked in red, on the back, "Beware of the bull".'

There were other times of fun and interest for Henbury villagers in war-time, Ray's recollections of his own social life give a flavour. There was the Carlton Cinema in Westbury on Trym, where he was always given a box of chocolates on entering (Black Magic, he thinks). Ray looked at his diary: 'On May 4th 1941, the Princess Royal [great aunt of the present one] visited the A.T.S. Centre at Mrs Gunn's house, Henbury House in Henbury Road.'

Ray had good friends in Brentry – the Lailleys, Frank and his wife and daughter, Peggy. Then there were the Tills and their daughter, Margy. Mrs Petit – another friend – had, Ray said, two smashing horses that he sometimes rode in shows. She also had a cocker spaniel that she wrote a book about. In the dark days people especially needed their friends. Morale had to be kept up!

The diary reminds Ray that 'the night that Mrs Biggs's hen house was set alight, I was at a dance at Henbury Court, where the Searchlight Brigade lived. It was commanded by Captain Bailley whose father owned the store of that name in Gloucester Road.

'About that time, our henhouse was inadvertently left open, with awful consequences. A fox got in and did its worst – such carnage! One of the hazards of farming, I'm afraid.'

Throughout those busy, troubled and stimulating times, the normal routine of farming proceeded, dictated not only by social and political affairs but inescapably by the seasons and the weather.

The cycle of farming events during peace and war was described in Chapter 4. But there were a few projects specific to war-time. Rationing included petrol. Farmer Ray soon had the idea of developing a kind of jaunting car, called a 'tub' outfit. It enabled farmers and other country people to get around their business and leisure pursuits without using up precious coupons. Farmer Ray bought old tub traps and had them repaired. Next, he bought and trained travelling ponies to pull them. They were then sold privately to interested people.

Another job, in common with neighbouring families, was to take in bed-and-breakfast boarders at about £3 per week. They were mostly students on the many war-time training courses.

Towards the end of the war, and shortly afterwards, there was some movement of households in Henbury. By 1950, the Old Crow had been taken over by landlord F.G. Jennison from landlord P. Tilly, at which time N.R. Gregory was landlord of the Salutation. In the centre of the village, Holly House, once the home of Smithy J. Grigg, became the home of Mrs Eve Hitching (later, the Browns) who kept a small shop there. Hillside and Beaconsfield had changed occupiers. The Hollies, Woodlands (now White Lodge) and Rose Bank had changed hands, and so had Henbury Lodge. There were a few changes in Wyck Beck Road, as well as at Westmoreland Cottage and Blaise Castle Lodge to mention only those known to us.

Perhaps the most interesting change was the arrival of Professor and Mrs Hewer in 1946, who took over Endcliffe and restored it to its original name, Vine House. Mrs Hewer is a daughter of Abigail Way of the old Vicarage Way family. Her arrival carried on a long tradition of Ways and their cousins, the Sampson-Ways as residents of Henbury.

The departure of long-standing neighbours is a cause of sadness as familiar faces are no longer seen in familiar places. But the newcomers who replace them, in time, promote new friendships and are accepted and no longer regarded as outsiders.

This terrible war caused departures much more devastating than a mere house move. Among the casualties of war, one of the best-known families of Henbury lost a son: Percy, son of Charles Newman of Raglan Villa. He had joined the R.A.F. and was killed in 1944 flying over Nuremburg. He left a wife and two small daughters. A friend of Farmer Ray, a butcher from Wrington, was killed. Wally Rudge and Dick Clifford (son of a Blaise Castle woodsman) were killed in the prime of life. Harold Godfrey has a photograph of them when they were members of the Henbury Robins Boys Football Team. The families of all these young men had the difficult job of learning to face life without them.

Farmer Ray recalls with sadness that in about 1940, Farmer Charles Rowley, his wife and son Jim were all killed by a direct hit on their air raid shelter on Charlton Common. On April 11th 1941, 180 people were killed in a heavy raid on Bristol. The farm vet survived but all his

Two of the Robins' football team of 1927–28, Dick Clifford and Wally Rudge, lost their lives in the second world war.

companions in the shelter died. From his diary, Ray noted that Winston Churchill visited the city the following day. He used to make a point of doing this after a heavy raid and his thoughtfulness helped to raise everyone's morale.

7 – After the war – peace?

At the beginning of 1945, there was a feeling that war was coming to an end, and before the end of May, war in Europe had indeed ended. On September 2nd, Japan's surrender was officially accepted by the Allies.

In villages and towns, relief from anxiety, overwork, drabness was everywhere apparent. First the lights went on and the 'blackouts' came down. Church bells rang out! Rationing remained for some time until food stocks could be replenished from renewed overseas trade. As building materials became available and craftsmen returned from the war, bomb damage was repaired, but this and new building took time.

Demobilisation of armed and other 'forces' commenced and thousands of young people returned to their family homes. Relationships and friendships had to be renewed. Many young sisters and brothers had grown to adulthood while their elders were away. After six years of normal progression on 'hold', there was a huge backlog of young people looking forward to settling down with a job, a home of their own, marriage and a family.

Farmer Ray explains how all this affected his family and others in Henbury. 'By now, I was myself married with a young son – the hope of every farmer is to see his son carry on his life's work. After the tremendous efforts of war-time farming, the farm was doing well. We now had one hundred head of cattle, three hundred pigs, three hundred head of sheep, one thousand hens in batteries, two tractors, two lorries, a motor car and motor bike. We had fifty acres growing corn and ten acres growing vegetables. We were renting a further forty acres of land and had grazing rights to Filton golf-course. The future looked good.

'For a year or two after war ended, we enjoyed our peace-time farming until in 1947 our landlord, Major Sampson-Way died. We were sorry because he had been a good landlord. But we were sorrier still when we heard that the Council wanted to compulsorily purchase our farm and others in order to carry out a programme of post-war housebuilding.' The surge of new young families formed after the war had become a national problem because of the country's depleted housing stock. This was partly because of the bombing but owed much more to the cessation of house-building during the war.

It seems that the farmland of Westmoreland and Norton Farms was heavily mortgaged and, with death duties, the Sampson-Way family would not have had a choice. In 1950, the farmer received a warning of the impending compulsory purchase. His first action was to speak to the other affected farmers, the Hignells and two Brentry farmers. Then they employed a barrister, but they had no chance against such authority and were given twelve months to quit land and farmstead.

Farmer Ray describes what then happened. 'We refused to quit the house and buildings, and eventually we got our own way as far as those were concerned. We were left with the small orchard behind the house, the house, the bakery, the stables and the tithe barn. I received £1,000 compensation but lost £7,000 or £8,000 through having to sell stock for what I could get for it, there was simply no time to wait for the right market!

'We then paid rent as council tenants which they kept increasing until soon I was paying the same amount I had paid the Major for the entire farmland! We suspected it might be a strategy to try to get rid of us.'

How did the Hignell family fare in all this? They suffered a similar shock from the compulsory purchase order; fortunately for them, it concerned only a section of their farm: the land south of the railway line, leaving them with the land north of the line – more than half their acreage.

As soon as they could, Clement and Tom bought this larger part from the Major's estate. When Clement died not long after this, Tom bought his father's share from his family. The old farmhouse was demolished in 1951, and the family went to live in North Hill Cottage, an old gamekeeper's cottage on their land. Tom and his wife were able to continue farming their land for many years until at last they retired.

The third Henbury village farm was also compulsorily purchased. The farmhouse, however, had been bought by the Biggs family many years before. Until the council started to redevelop their farmland, they continued to graze their cows for some time, but only on a short-term basis.

For the first time, they realised the implication of ceasing to be Gloucestershire people and becoming an adjunct of Bristol.

The new development starts

Farmer Ray describes the process. 'The Council proceeded to plan alterations to the route of Crow Lane for easier access to the houses and shops they were going to build on my farm and on the Hignells' farm. These farms had been there for centuries with field names, some of which had been handed down by families for generations. These were to lose their identity and boundaries to the march of 'progress'. They had never ceased to be viable food producers, memories must be short,

'We needed security for
our family.'

'The hope of every
farmer is to see his son
carrying on his life's
work.

especially war-memories!

'The first nuisance was road-widening and the demolition of our garden wall abutting Crow Lane. It was replaced about ten feet nearer to the house and a pavement added. The dust, noise and chaos were indescribable!

'As the houses went up progressively, I managed to get the council to rent back some of my land to me on a temporary basis. No longer could I build up herds, the outlook was bleak, the future always now had to be short-term. So I fatted up stock, kept a few pigs, dug a kitchen garden in part of the orchard, started a small farm shop and kept a few chickens.

'The landscape changed as Crow Lane was brought nearer to us and straightened out. The oak tree in front of the houses beyond Blaise Primary School and behind the 'green' is the daughter of an oak tree that I allowed to grow many years earlier in my hedge alongside Crow Lane when it was a farm lane. That tree gives you an idea of the route of the original lane. We used to make hay beside the old oak and we have a snapshot of us building a hay rick there.

'We wondered at the time if the ever-increasing rent was intended to get us out of the house so that they could demolish it (as at Norton) for further building development. Added to this, our repeated requests to buy the house were turned down. We needed security for our family, now a boy and a girl, and another in the future. Somehow, we survived, managing to make ends meet and bring up our three children.

'From then on, my farming career was patchy and varied, but, with additional enterprises, we coped – and launched our children into successful adulthood. Then at long last, in the late seventies/early eighties when council tenants were allowed to buy their rented houses, we bought ours.

'Some of The Elms was developed into housing areas, some was kept as playing fields. The farms in Brentry suffered a similar fate to ours.

Scattered round modern Henbury are practical reminders of earlier times, such as street names, house names. In the final chapter of Part Two, some of these are described together with old field names of Norton and Westmoreland Farms.

Perhaps the 'new' villagers of Henbury and Brentry can spare a sympathetic thought for the bitterness the farmers felt at that time. We bear no grudges now – we are older and we hope, wiser. I should, however, like to feel that the present Henbury residents know about the farming heritage of their village. This book, we hope, will have contributed a little towards that end.'

Preface

In writing the second part of this book, we are aware that the period, places and events are similar to those in Part One. It seems unnecessary to retell all the details of the farming year, methods of farming, the changing modes of operation over time and through social and political upheaval.

Instead, we concentrate on the farmers and their families, their ambitions and life-styles. One catches a glimpse of Tom Hignell, steeped in his love of animals, of the countryside and its people and of his vocation in farming. There is always a smile lurking in the corners of his mouth, and you know a story is about to come tumbling out, while Robert Biggs' serious, dignified presence conceals a dry sense of humour and the memory of a life of a hard-working farmer.

The three farming families knew and liked each other, co-operating in many ways down succeeding generations in business and in their social lives.

Just as they complemented each other's farming activities, so their personalities were complementary. There appears to have been no rivalry, and plenty of empathy.

Part Two opens with a look at country life in the early days of Tom and Robert.

Many residents of old Henbury still alive and well today, who were born before or between the two world wars, can remember their country childhood. The village, containing within its boundaries three farms, was surrounded also by other villages and farmland. To north, south, east and west, a swathe of green rippled from Avonmouth to Filton, much of which was part of Gloucestershire.

Those were the days when passengers and freight were carried between Filton and Avonmouth on a branch line of the G.W.R. – still running today, but no longer the old G.W.R. and no longer offering a passenger service.

The nearest large village was Westbury on Trym. Apart from a few grand houses, Westbury and Henbury were joined (and separated) by the hill and its farmlands. Most people had to walk or cycle into Westbury to visit the shops. They could then board a tram at the terminus by Mogford's Ironmongery and travel into the city and its suburbs.

Some of the Westbury grocers' shops provided a weekly delivery service by horse-drawn cart or van. To supplement this, Henbury's own small shop was most useful.

The Biggs family farm delivered its produce by horse-drawn vans. A baker brought his horse-drawn cobern round the village on a regular basis. From the station yard, great horses pulled coal-carts to supply householders with fuel for heating and cooking. Everyone had a coal fire and many had coal-fired ovens and ranges.

Horses abounded. It was common to see a horse, awaiting the return of its driver, eating from a bag suspended from its head-harness. Later, when motor-traffic was in use alongside horse-drawn vehicles, many horses were provided with 'blinkers' – shields to reduce the effect on the animals of cars speeding by.

It was into this environment that Robert Biggs was born, and in which he and Tom Hignell grew up in the 1920s.

There have been farms in Henbury Village for many hundreds of years. It is likely that their names – Norton, Westmoreland and The Elms – have remained unchanged for the whole of that time. The first part of this book records farm work and life in the last decades of Henbury as a farming village, from the memories of the McEwen Smiths of Westmoreland Farm. Part two is compiled from the memories of Tom Hignell of Norton Farm and Robert Biggs of The Elms Dairy Farm. The period covered is dictated by what they remember of their time in farming and what they knew from their parents. This is roughly the first half of this century.

Tom Hignell and Robert Biggs grew up on their farms and attended schools nearby, though not in the village. They have contributed information about the village as they remembered it in their childhood, about family outings, church life and growing up. In both men, the influence of their farm upbringing was profound, though manifesting in different ways. Tom took over from his father very early as his father's health gave way. After the war, he ran the farm on his own. Robert worked with his father for some years. Much later after the war, he ran another family farm to the west of Bristol.

Their careers were affected by the compulsory purchase order, but in different ways from each other and from the McEwen Smiths. This will become clear as the narrative progresses.

1 – The Hignells of Norton Farm

It is no longer possible to see Norton Farmhouse, but one can get some idea of its appearance from photographs. As it has many similarities to the later wing of Westmoreland Farmhouse, it would be fair to date Norton to the early 1800s. However, Norton Farm is mentioned much earlier than that in old Henbury documents, indicating an earlier building. Tom Hignell recalls that there was an inner part of the house at a different level – probably the older house.

With almost 190 acres, Norton was the largest of the three farms in the village. Just under half of this lay south of the railway line. The rest reached up to Haw Wood and Mount Skitham. From west to east it stretched from Ison or Piddly Hill to the farms at the west of Charlton Village. There were also a few fields between Station Road and the Hazel Brook.

The Hignells ran a mixed farming economy that will be described during the story. Some of the fields had interesting names, and these, too, will be explained all in good time.

In 1917, a young family who had been farming in Lawrence Weston moved into Henbury. Both husband and wife were from farming families going back for generations. Clement Hignell and his wife took over the tenancy of Norton Farm from the landlord, General Sampson-Way. They brought with them vast farming experience, a daughter, Alice Hannah and two small sons, Tom and Bob.

Tom, the elder boy, was four years old at the time. He soon started school at a kindergarten (now no more) behind the Glen by Blackboy Hill in Bristol. Bob soon joined him, and in due time both progressed to Redland Hill House School. When they weren't occupied with school and church activities, they spent most of their time playing together on the farm and with the animals.

As Tom grew into his 'teens, his father Clem was becoming crippled, suffering great pain from the onset of arthritis. So it was decided that Tom should be withdrawn from school at the age of thirteen or fourteen to help with the heavy work of the farm. It doesn't seem to have been a hardship to Tom who, from a young age, loved and cared for animals, and found complete happiness and satisfaction in rural pursuits and the farming way of life. In course of time, Bob joined his brother, and with the help of two farm workers, the family worked the farm between them.

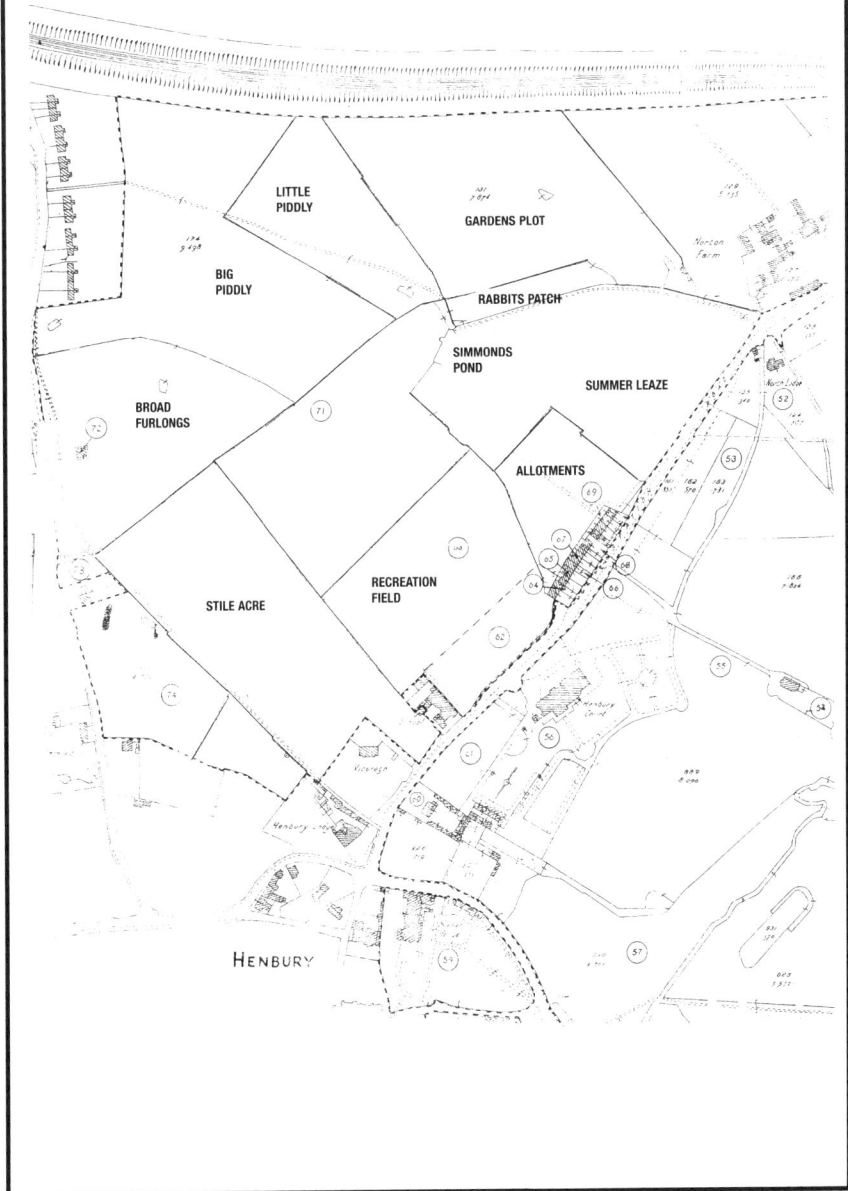

Norton Farm

LITTLE PIDDLY

GARDENS PLOT

BIG PIDDLY

RABBITS PATCH

SIMMONDS POND

SUMMER LEAZE

BROAD FURLONGS

ALLOTMENTS

STILE ACRE

RECREATION FIELD

HENBURY

By the time their neighbour, young Farmer Ray arrived in the village to start his farming career at Westmoreland Farm, Norton Farm was already mature and thriving under the care of the four Hignells.

Blacksmith at Norton Farm, 1956.

Hignell horse and cart.

2 – Norton Farm in the Thirties

Tom Hignell talks about their farming in the thirties. 'By 1930, Dad owned about one hundred sheep and about forty milk cows and sixty other cattle – beef and calves. He also had the usual chickens, ducks and turkeys, all "free-range" of course, pecking their way round the farmyard. In the years following, we also had two hundred sheep in Blaise Castle Park. The two ha-has in the Park, now removed, were essential then.

'I remember red squirrels at Echo Gate. I also clearly remember the occasion when our sheep, grazing on the Park, pushed their way through a hedge and swiped somebody's crop of mangolds and swedes!

'Another time, police woke us at 2 a.m. one night to tell us that our sheep were in the road, and that they had shut them in the churchyard. Would we collect them immediately, please? I got out of bed, pulled some clothes on drowsily and went to rescue the sheep. I herded them temporarily into one of our yards – and went back to bed. In the morning, I was wakened by Dad's voice calling out, "Just come down and look, we've got a strange flock of sheep in the yard!"

'Bob and I did our own sheep-shearing under instruction from father. We never did our own slaughtering, though, but sent stock for sale to private butchers, who of course did the slaughtering. We did not bake our own bread, nor make butter or cheese for sale, only for home consumption. I believe the McEwen Smiths followed this practice also. Probably time was more efficiently spent on other things, bearing in mind the mechanised dairy factories and bakeries then prevalent. We sold some of our milk, however, to Stan Biggs for his milk 'round'.

'In the thirties, we used horses round the farm like most other farmers. We had five horses including a brood mare; and these five pulled plough, mower, harrows, hay carts and market carts.

'As you would expect from a large acreage of pasture, we collected a good deal of hay. By 1930, Dad had a dutch barn to store it in. Prior to that he just had haystacks and cornstacks in traditional style. The hay was used mostly for feeding our own stock and the corn straw was for bedding the stock. The main cash crop was wheat. We also grew potatoes, mangolds and kale.'

It was in the 1930s, as Westbury was greatly expanding with housing developments, that their way of life began to change. As Westbury spread out from its village centre, it brought more townsfolk into closer proximity with the countryside and its written and unwritten rules. Tom says, 'I remember a man who owned greyhounds and did not keep them under control. We lost twenty two sheep to the ravages of these dogs.'

'A similar tragedy happened to sheep grazing over the underground petrol tanks, north of the railway line. Three little terriers tore the flesh off the faces of seven ewes and ate a lately-delivered lamb. The lamb's mother went into a decline and off her food, dying of what I would call a broken heart.

'There was a distressing sequel to that occurrence when an un-neighbourly watchman phoned the police and reported my pining sheep instead of phoning me. I was reported as 'uncaring' – when I have spent my life caring for animals. As a direct result, I sold my sheep and decided not to rear them again!'

Tom Hignell and family.

3 – War-time farming

'Towards the end of the thirties, Dad and I introduced automatic milking. As war started in 1939, we changed from horse power to engine power. As the horses went out, so less labour was needed. Engines don't need the level of care that farmers give to their horses. In many ways they, that is, engines are more efficient.

'War progressed and the government demanded more food from British farmers in order to be self-sufficient and avoid using imported food. The ships carrying this food were very vulnerable to enemy attack. Norton Farm increased arable, and we ploughed up fields for cereal-growing. These included Big Hawleaze, the field next to six acres and other fields west of Mount Skitham. We bought a tractor to help with the increased ploughing.

'We also kept pigs during the war, a quick way of producing the extra meat needed. For the feed, we kept a boiler in the courtyard and, like Ray and many other farmers, we collected food waste from surrounding kitchens, canteens, hotels and so on.

'Then the farm workers were called up to the armed services and land girls joined Norton Farm. We had two very helpful girls but to begin with every job on the farm made their backs ache!

'I want to tell you about my cattle next. Bulls can be mild and friendly creatures. My Hereford bull in its pen would put its head over the fence for you to give it a friendly scratch of its curly head. We called him 'Noddy'. Now, Friesian and Hereford bulls will fight each other. But in general, Herefords which are bred for beef are docile creatures; whereas Jerseys and Guernseys, which are bred for milk, are much more vicious. So how do you explain that?

'Management of breeding cattle is all-important. At Norton, the milking cows were kept in fields near to the farmstead and milking parlours, for they were milked twice each day. For breeding beef calves, when half a dozen heifers were ready, they were taken to Mount Skitham where the Hereford bull was kept. (Every now and then the bull broke through the hedge at Mt Skitham and returned itself to its pen – as if it was all too much!)

'For breeding milk calves, heifers that were ready were treated by artificial insemination from Channel Island or Friesian bulls.'

Norton Farm, with Mr and Mrs Tom Hignell.

4 – Social Life

In between the demands of farm work, farming families attended the Parish Church where they met each other and other village friends. Tom says, 'Our family have always been keen supporters of St. Mary's Parish Church in Henbury. We have involved ourselves in the social life of the church too, such as the Mothers' Union, the choir, Communicants' Guild. Some of us joined the Henbury Drama Club held at the village school. Sometimes we attended whist drives. Some leisure pursuits outside the village were the cinema, and ballroom dancing at the local Young Farmers Club at Olveston.

'We were customers of the village shops and businesses, and the Post Office, another place for seeing friends. For getting about locally, we went by bike or on foot.'

The Hignells were a busy, active family. Farming was in their blood and a way of life inherited from generations of farming folk. They, like the McEwen Smiths and the Biggs family, joined in agricultural shows and competitions, great family outings where they entered themselves and their animals and produce in various 'classes', sometimes winning, sometimes losing. But it was all good fun, gave them targets to work for, gave them new ideas. Farming can be an isolated way of life, so such events were a welcome break and an opportunity to meet old friends. There were also fairs, markets and horse-shows.

In 1944, Tom married. He and his parents then divided the farmhouse into two parts. At the same time they became joint tenants of Major (son of General) Sampson-Way, continuing to run the farm together. Bob, the younger son lived with his parents until he was married, when he procured the lease of a farm on the banks of the river Trym between Westbury and Southmead Village.

After the war came to an end they, like the other farmers in Henbury (and in Brentry) suffered a shattering blow to their way of life and farming.

5 – The end of the war

The farmers' war effort had meant tremendously hard work and no 'let up'. They had been aware of being within a wider war-effort as well. The village was filled with army men and women, there was an anti-aircraft unit and a searchlight unit not many yards away from the farmhouse. There was heavy bombing of nearby Bristol, Avonmouth and Filton. Even Henbury had been bombed and fires started. There had been restrictions and shortages. The farmers, the villagers, the service personnel all had put their backs into the fight – the fight for freedom.

As 1945 dawned and launched into Spring, there was a sense of impending peace. For the first time in six years, people could start to relax. They could also start to plan for the future. Farmers hoped to be able to return to a regime where they would do their own planning.

For a time their lives seemed to be returning to normal and for about five years their progress was going according to plan – their own plan! But national and local government plans were also proceeding – to house the returning service people and the new young families.

By 1950, the farmers of Henbury and Brentry had been warned of an order to compulsorily purchase the farmland. They joined together to employ a barrister to represent them but to no avail.

The other farmers lost all their land but the Hignell family lost only about half of theirs. The CPO did not include the land north of the railway line and as the death of their landlord, Major Sampson-Way had precipitated the compulsory purchase, they then set about buying the northern section of their farm from the Major's estate.

When Clement died not long after this, Tom bought his father's share from the family. The farmhouse was demolished in 1951 and they went to live in North Hill Cottage, an old game-keeper's cottage on their land.

They were able, Tom and his wife, to continue farming their land for many years after this until at last they retired.

6 – The Biggs Family of The Elms Dairy Farm

Looking down over the village from the top of Henbury hill, The Elms Dairy Farm could be seen on the right hand side reaching down from Sheep Wood under the ridge to the bottom of the hill and the farmhouse. To the east, it was separated by a line of hedging from Westmoreland farmland. This line of hedging came back to The Elms Farmhouse. To protect the cows and their pastureland of thirty acres, a strong hedge and ditching ran along the roadside. A further ten acres of grassland were rented to make up a total of forty acres. These were the show ground behind Westmoreland Farmhouse, and pasture near Blaise Hamlet.

The Elms Farmhouse, situated close to the road with windows overlooking the grazing land, was a roomy gabled and attractive family house dating, according to Robert Biggs, from the reign of Queen Anne.

For more than fifty years, the Biggs family worked The Elms Dairy Farm. The farm was widely known in Henbury, in neighbouring villages and in Bristol suburbs because of its large milk round and Channel Island milk. From their relatively small pasture, delectable dairy products were delivered to doorsteps to give nourishment and pleasure to hundreds of families.

Mr Robert Biggs tells of his family's history. 'The first of the Biggs family to arrive in Henbury were William and Louisa, who took up the tenancy of the farm from the owner, Mr Levy Langfield in about 1900. William and Louisa had five sons, at least some of whom were born before the family's arrival in Henbury because my father, Stan was thirteen years old in 1900. Two of the brothers emigrated to America. Another brother, Harold lost a leg in the first world war; the youngest, Victor had a successful career in insurance.

'After the death of my grandfather William in 1911, father, then aged twenty four, took over the tenancy. Seven years later he married my mother, Hilda Rowles, the daughter of a Brentry farming family.

'In about 1920, Mr Somerville Gunn of Henbury House bought The Elms farmland from Mr Langfield. At the same time my father, Stan bought the farmhouse.

'Father started his farming with a herd of Shorthorns, but his ambition was to build up a herd entirely of Guernseys. By 1930, he had twenty-two cows including ten Guernseys and two Jerseys. By the end of that decade, he had achieved his ambition, owning a herd of thirty Guernseys. He maintained this size of herd throughout the war and later by breeding his own cattle, disposing of the male calves, and keeping the best of the heifers to replenish the herd.

'Because his milk rounds also carried other than Channel Island milk, he bought in what he needed from other local farmers, including Clem Hignell of Norton Farm.'

The farm dairy was situated at the far end of the farmhouse, away from the road. It is interesting to read an extract from a reprint from *Town and Country News* for December 18th 1931:

> In every detail this dairy is completely up-to-date, the most approved modern plant and equipment having been installed, including a J&E Hall electric refrigerator, electric bottle-washing machines, electric separator, and a steam boiler for sterilizing purposes, also plant for making clotted cream. The strictest cleanliness is maintained throughout, and the milk is handled as little as possible, thereby reaching the consumer in as fresh and cleanly condition as is humanly possible.

and further: 'The cow houses are fitted with automatic drinking bowls, to ensure a clean supply of water for each cow.'

Milk and other dairy products were delivered to doorsteps in the early days by three roundsmen driving horse-drawn vans. By 1931, motorised vans were being used by The Elms (probably among the earliest farms to use them). The number increased over the years until twenty roundsmen went out every day.

Robert Biggs continues, 'From the forty acres of grassland, they were able to graze the cows and also to make enough hay for the cattle to eat during the winter months. This hay was stored in barns including a dutch barn situated down the hill from the house, roughly about where the new houses of Trym Close now stand.

'Other enterprises included a large number of Rhode Island Red poultry, the eggs taking prizes at local shows. And of course, there was the vegetable garden for home-consumption. Vegetables were grown in a large walled garden behind the house. (The wall was demolished when Trym Close was built.) 'In about 1930, Mr Gunn built the bungalow (behind Elm Cottages) to house his groom.'

Elms Dairy Farm in the 1930s.

Motorised milk delivery vans were in use by 1931. At one stage, 20 roundsmen went out every day.

7 – Social Cohesion

Robert recalls tales of his parents' youth

The Biggs family seem to have led a busy, successful, hard-working life, but no-one exists in isolation. What about their social life and relationships with neighbours and friends? We already know from several other residents of old Henbury as well as from Robert that the church of St Mary was well-attended. We know also that a good deal of friendly contact was maintained through church services, and the numerous church social events. These activities seem to have provided the means of unifying the village, giving it identity and social stability.

But as well as this cohesion through the church, there were many other contacts and friendships at different age levels and interests. Robert remembers that there had been a tennis club over at Westmoreland Farm, on Home Field when his aunts were young. His mother and her sisters, the Rowles of Brentry were friends of the McEwen Smith sisters round about the time of the first world war. The Hort girls of Fane Cottage were also among their group of friends. They would play tennis together, meet at church, social events, dances and visit each other's homes. (Years later, the tennis court was rediscovered and brought into use by Ray and his aunt.) Stan Biggs was at one time the tennis club chairman and secretary. Later still the Biggs family made a court in their own garden.

Robert's Generation

Life proceeded for the family with hard work and good results throughout the pre-war days. Stan and Hilda's sons, Robert and John were growing up. The boys started their schooling at a pre-preparatory school at Cribbs Causeway. Then in turn, they graduated to a preparatory school in Westbury Road, Westbury on Trym. (The house is now used by the Conservative Party for their local office.) When he was a little older, Robert attended Bristol Grammar School. By then he was riding to school on his bicycle, joined a few years later by his brother John.

At the Grammar School, Robert was introduced to rugby and cricket. He remembers also playing cricket on the lawn of Henbury Vicarage with the son of the vicar, the Reverend John Collins Lloyd.

Robert reminisces: 'I had many relatives and friends in the farming community and when young, played with my brother on our own or other people's farms. For instance, it was fun to put a raft on the Hazel Brook behind Westmoreland Farmhouse.' He cycled around as he grew older, and his school and games kept him occupied. As a country boy, there were farming events such as agricultural shows to enjoy. At the Henbury showground there was an annual flower show and an annual horse show was held in a field behind Henbury Court, as well as other shows further afield. There were country markets and fairs, too.

As Robert grew older, there were dances and clubs to join, political parties and 'functions'. And 'When I was old enough, I'd enjoy my pint of Bass at the Salutation'.

Shortly after the war, Robert married and after living in a flat at the top of the farmhouse, bought the bungalow that Mr Gunn had built some years before for his groom. Robert enlarged it to make a family-sized house for himself and his wife.

The war years

Robert recalls that families were exhorted to collect tinned and other preserved foods in order to establish an emergency store cupboard. Families with at least one child under fourteen were issued with a small family-sized air-raid shelter. Everyone else was encouraged to prepare make-shift shelters under such places as stairs or a heavy table.

Like Farmer Ray, Robert well remembers the air raid wardens, and that the church bells were silenced and held in reserve for possible warning against enemy invasion. Fortunately, the only invasion that Henbury saw was the arrival of army personnel to man a searchlight battery on the Arthur Baker Memorial Ground, and an anti-aircraft gun emplacement across the brook behind Westmoreland Farmhouse. Robert remembers that, later in the war, the American army replaced the British – a new experience for the villagers, especially as there were various ethnic groups among the GIs.

When the farm labourers were called up, the Biggs, like other farmers, employed landgirls, mostly from the Women's Land Army. Their work was invaluable and enabled the farm to continue its high standard and output. There were probably about eight girls, though not all at the same time.

After the war

Mr Gunn's land, The Elms, was also subject to a compulsory

purchase. However, for some time after this, cows continued to graze the pasture that became to a large extent the village recreation field, when the house-building was completed.

Stan Biggs died in December, 1962, leaving his two sons, Robert and John. John, who farmed at Fowey in Cornwall, died there in 1979.

After the compulsory purchase of the farm land they had leased from Mr Gunn, Robert had bought a family farm at West End, Nailsea in Somerset, where he continued the excellent standard developed by his father, Stan in Henbury. At Robert's farm, his cows grazed contentedly and produced good milk there just as they had done in Henbury. And in like manner, Robert sent his dairy-produce forth on 'rounds' for the benefit of the surrounding families.

8 – Names to intrigue

When one considers the antiquity of Henbury, names come to mind, names that have a meaning or an allusion to something or someone long forgotten.

Starting with Westmoreland Farm fields, consider Top Field or Lookout Field. These names refer to its position at the top of the land under the Ridgeway, and also to the nickname given to the ruined window.

Dragonswell Field may have derived its name from a warm spring in a pond there that never froze over.

Farmer Ray says his Alley Field got its name from the narrow alley beside Harry Hignell's house and shop, giving a short cut into Passage Road. (There were several cottages along that piece of Passage Road.)

Home Field is next to the homestead.

Lily Pond Field explains itself.

Trapstyle Field had a trap style into Crow Lane. It was intended to trap in the animals, but you had to look out for yourself. You had to press it down to go through, and a counterweight brought it back up again. Woe betide anyone who let go too soon!

To continue: Wyck Field was close to Wyck House.

The name 'Pool Leaze' is very old but Farmer Ray does not know its origin. He further tells me that fields named by acreage do not always reflect actual size.

It is interesting to know how the tithing map of 1839 labels these same fields. To begin with, the orchard was the same in 1839. Lily Pond Field was merely numbered 595 on the tithe map. Home Field was known as Home Ground. 12 acre Field was known as Horts Ground or Brentry. Dragonswell was Little Mead or Quarry Ground. Top Field was Long Hill, Lookout was 5 acres. Part of Lookout may have been Calves Leaze. Trapstyle was Furlongs. 16 acre was part of Wick Mead. Pool Leaze remained the same. Alley used to be Westbury on Trym Ground.

Long Hill, the old name, was probably so named because it was felt to be a long pull-up when hand ploughing.

Calves Leaze was probably where calves were separated out of the herd when they were weaned. Quarry Ground may be a name given to the field because it was near the quarry. (along Passage Road)

Looking now at the Hignells' land on Norton Farm, one sees Big

1990 Current housing and the farms as they were

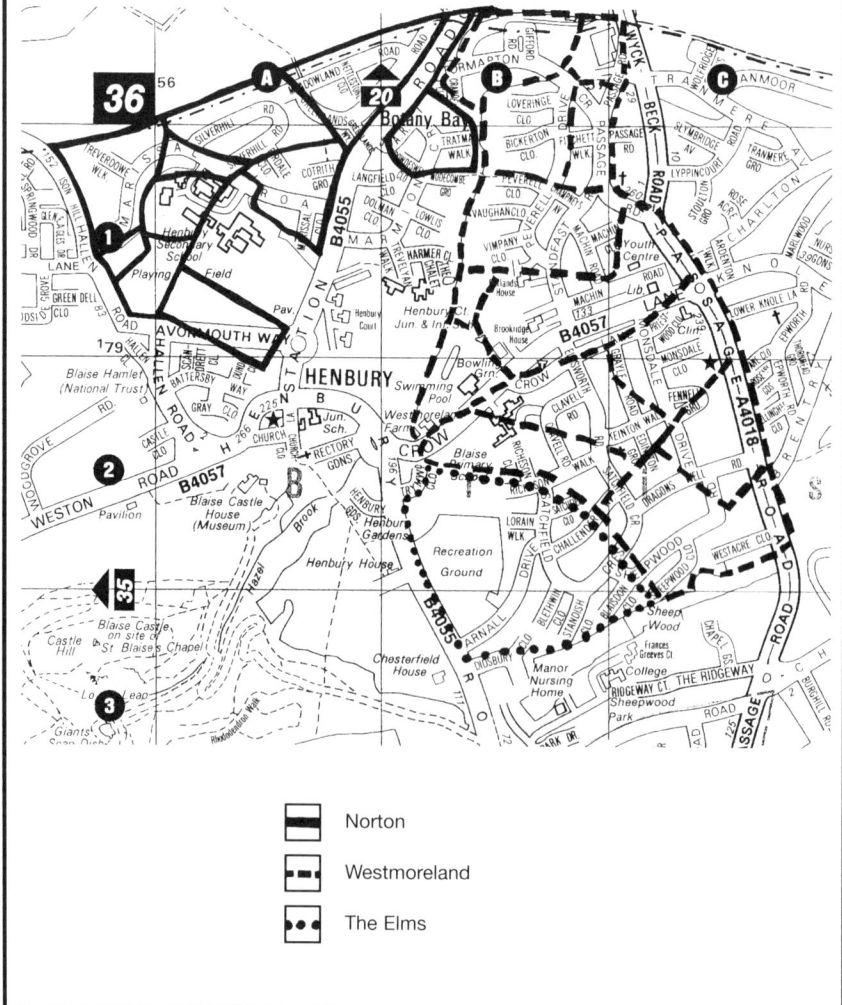

	Norton
	Westmoreland
	The Elms

Piddly and Little Piddly, so called, according to Farmer Tom Hignell, because they were often wet! Farmers, I have discovered, like to tease; and if they don't know the answer to a question are liable to manufacture one on the spot.

So to look at the next one – Gardensplott – perhaps they grew vegetables there? Where the branch line Filton to Avonmouth meets the branch line Pilning to Avonmouth, there are a number of farms with 'splot' as part of their name.

Greenhill explains itself. Calves Hill – similar to Calves Leaze, we think. North Hill is geographical. Station Ground – next to Railway Station, and Wyck & Home Field as in Westmoreland Farm.

Top Hawleaze and Big Hawleaze are near to Haw Wood. The W.I. Guide to Henbury informs one that a 'haw' was a strong fence enclosing woodland which contained wild animals, in time it came to mean the woodland itself.

Stileacre had a footpath across it with a stile each end – according to Farmer Tom's memory, they were actually kissing gates.

The name 'Blaise' is a reference to St Blaise who is popularly known as the patron saint of wool combers. One reads in the W.I. Guide that St Blaise was 'a lover of solitude, and wild animals'.

Norton Farm is mentioned in ancient documents – for instance, in a bundle presented to the Bristol Record Office by the Diocesan Registrar, there is a reference in 1675 to lands 'now in possession of widow Norton', referring to Henbury Parish.

Westmoreland and Fane have a close connection. Fane was and still is the family name of the Earls of Westmoreland. The Fane family owned tithings in Henbury from the seventeenth century. At the back of Westbury Parish Church there is a board of historical data, including '. . . on 2nd November 1669 Sir Francis Fane patron of the living granted to John Willoughby and others and their heirs for ever the tithes of Pen Park of one farm thereon and of one "Conigree" in trust to secure to the vicar of Westbury on Trym a stipend of £10 per annum for ever.' It seems that 'Alley Field', one-time Westbury on Trym Ground was not the only gift to Westbury Parish Church.

We can now look at modern post-1950 Henbury road names. Trevelyan Walk reminds us that Walter Trevelyan was a vicar of St Mary's Henbury in the nineteenth century.

Scandrett Close – John Scandrett Harford built Blaise Castle House. His son had the same name, while John Battersby Harford was obviously the inspiration for Battersby Way.

Vimpany was a surname in the Henbury Church Registers in around 1590.

Loveringe Close is a reminder of Sarah Loveringe, an eighteenth-century matron to the 'Blue Boys' of Anthony Edmonds School who boarded at Close House.

Levy Langfield at one time owned Henbury Court Hotel, and so we see Langfield Close not far from the site of the hotel.

Moving over to Ison Hill, Windmill Lane is not far from the site of a windmill. Hill End Drive leads to the site of Hill End House. This large house with its gardens and small farm was owned by Captain Gilbert James, who kept a herd of pedigree Jerseys and a milking parlour. The farm was managed by Mr Arthur Hawkins who still lives in the Lodge in Windmill Lane close to Hill End Drive. Convent Close is a further reminder of the fairly recent history of Hill End House. For some years before the modern housing was built, the Sisters of the Convent of the Good Shepherd used the big house as a rehabilitation centre for young girls.

Passage Road is still very much in the present, though somewhat modified in its route. It of course reminds everyone of the ferry to Wales, of which Samuel Rudder wrote:

> In this parish are two ferries over the Severn. The uppermost, or Old Passage, is in the tithing of Aust, thirteen miles on a turn-pike road from Bristol. There the river is above two miles over, and the opposite house is at Beachley in the parish of Tidenham in this county (Gloucestershire). The other ferry, called the New Passage, is at Redwick, about three miles further down the river, and eleven miles distant from Bristol. There the water is about three miles over; and the opposite passage-house is at a place called the Black Rock, near St. Pierre's in Monmouthshire.
>
> *A New History of Gloucestershire*, first published 1779.

Maps

We have included nine maps in this book. That of 1990 shows the old farms superimposed on present day housing.

Everyone, I believe, agrees that Henbury is a delightful place to live in. We have the park and woods of Blaise Castle Estate. We have public grasslands alongside Henbury Hill, on both sides. There are the fields and hedgerows beside the Hazel Brook. In addition to these natural leisure places, we have a swimming bath, shops, health centre and library. In our own homes, we have up-to-date equipment. So we can enjoy the benefits of both ancient and modern.

The future nowadays is only too unpredictable. In thinking about the past, it is possible to get a sense of stability, continuity. But if we dwell on the past as some 'Utopia', we could become discontented with the present and fall into the 'good old days' trap.

The present and future demand that we bestir ourselves in order to shape them. If, then, present and future are 'dynamic' why concern oneself at all with the past - we cannot alter it, it is dead and dusty!

The past, however, created the present. What kind of a world did our predecessors inherit and what sort of a job did they make of it? If we can answer these questions, it may help us in creating the future.

I am sure that the ghosts of 'Henbury Past' are smiling down on us, the people of 'Henbury Present'. We are the modern villagers of Henbury. I believe they are wishing us well.

Resources for 'The Lost Farms of Henbury'

The authors wish to acknowledge with thanks the help derived from the following:

Eveleigh D. *A Popular Retreat* City of Bristol Museum and Art Gallery and Kingsmead Press 1987

Hallen and Henbury Women's Institute *A Guide to Henbury* printer: F. Bailey & Son Ltd Dursley 1970

Layzell Doreen *Invitation to Henbury* Redcliffe Press Ltd Bristol 1984

Rudder S. *A New History of Gloucestershire* First published 1779

Photographs have been kindly lent by R. McEwen Smith, D. Hellen, H. Godfrey and T. Hignell.

Henbury Parish Church
Pamphlet "St. Mary's Church Henbury A Brief History."
Memorial tablets – inside. Gravestones – outside. Church architecture.

Bristol Central Library
Street Directories

Henbury Library
General reading and use of photocopier

Bristol Records Office
Henbury tithing maps, rates books, church registers and records.

Bristol Diocesan Office
Maps of Henbury Parish

Rural History Centre University of Reading four photographs: winged plough, crank axle cattle cart, crank axle cart and bow rave wagon.

Information from residents of 'Old Henbury'.